God's Address—
Living with the Triune God

God's Address—
Living with the Triune God

A Scripture Workbook in the Style of Manuduction
to Accompany *The Lion, the Dove, & the Lamb*

REVISED EDITION

A. BRYDEN BLACK

WIPF & STOCK · Eugene, Oregon

GOD'S ADDRESS—LIVING WITH THE TRIUNE GOD,
REVISED EDITION
A Scripture Workbook in the Style of Manuduction to Accompany *The Lion, the Dove, & the Lamb*

Copyright © 2019 A. Bryden Black. All rights reserved. Except for brief quotations in critical publications or reviews, no part of this book may be reproduced in any manner without prior written permission from the publisher. Write: Permissions, Wipf and Stock Publishers, 199 W. 8th Ave., Suite 3, Eugene, OR 97401.

Wipf & Stock
An Imprint of Wipf and Stock Publishers
199 W. 8th Ave., Suite 3
Eugene, OR 97401

www.wipfandstock.com

PAPERBACK ISBN: 978-1-5326-8492-0
HARDCOVER ISBN: 978-1-5326-8493-7
EBOOK ISBN: 978-1-5326-8494-4

Manufactured in the U.S.A.   MARCH 27, 2019

For our grandchildren, Rachel, Peter, and Charlotte. May the prayer of Eph 3:14–21 truly become yours as Big Papa grants you his fulsome answers.

When Jesus turned and saw them following, he said to them, "What are you looking for?" They said to him, "Rabbi" (which translated means Teacher), "where are you staying?" He said to them, "Come and see."

(JOHN 1:38–39 NRSV)

Contents

List of Illustrations | ix
Permissions | x
Preface | xi
Acknowledgments | xiii
Further Acknowledgments | xiv
Abbreviations | xv

Introduction | 1

Part One (Session 1)
    The Story Unfolds: Abraham to Exile | 6

Part One (Session 2)
    Get Ready! The Day of Yahweh | 11

Part Two (Session 3)
    Ready for What? For Whom? Jesus' Coming | 18

Part Three (Session 4)
    Full Immersion in the Rule of God's Life: Luke–Acts | 26

Part Three (Session 5)
    Abiding in the Rule of God's Life: Baptism and Eucharist | 31

Contents

Part Four (Session 6)

    Growing into the Fullness of God's Life: Ephesians 1–3 | 37

Part Four (Session 7)

    Growing into the Fullness of God's Life: The NT Catechism | 44

Part Four (Session 8)

    Growing into the Fullness of God's Life: The Catechism continues | 52

Part Five (Session 9)

    God's Faithfulness in Overflowing Life: Galatians 3:1–4:7 | 57

Conclusion | 67

A Closing Prayer (Karl Barth, 1886-1968) | 70
Notes for Leaders | 71
A Covenant Summary | 75
A Way of "Reading" the Sacrament of the Eucharist | 84
Summary Chart of the One Baptism | 89
Bibliography | 91

List of Illustrations

Figure 1   Israel's Future Hope | 11
Figure 2   Israel's Future Hope (once more) | 21
Figure 3   The Christian Fulfilment | 22
Figure 4   A representation of the Economy derived from Luke–Acts | 27
Figure 5   The Christian Fulfilment (once more) | 29
Figure 6   Luke–Acts revised displaying both dominical sacraments | 31
Figure 7   *Andrei Rublev's icon of the Three Angels of Mamre*, 1410 | 66
Figure 8   Luke–Acts revised displaying both dominical sacraments | 88

Permissions

Bible translations are from the following, as marked:

Scripture quotations marked (NRSV) are taken from the New Revised Standard Version Bible, copyright © 1989, Division of Christian Education of the National Council of the Churches of Christ in the United States of America. Used by permission. All rights reserved.

Scripture quotations marked (NIV) are taken from the Holy Bible, New International Version®, NIV®. Copyright © 1973, 1978, 1984, 2011 by Biblica, Inc.T Used by permission of Zondervan. All rights reserved worldwide. www.zondervan.com The "NIV" and "New International Version" are trademarks registered in the United States Patent and Trademark Office by Biblica, Inc.T.

Scripture quotations marked (ESV) are from the ESV® Bible (The Holy Bible, English Standard Version®), copyright © 2001 by Crossway, a publishing ministry of Good News Publishers. Used by permission. All rights reserved.

Scripture quotations marked (RSV) are from the Revised Standard Version of the Bible, copyright © 1946, 1952, and 1971 the Division of Christian Education of the National Council of the Churches of Christ in the United States of America. Used by permission. All rights reserved.

Scripture quotations marked (NLT) are taken from the Holy Bible, New Living Translation, copyright ©1996, 2004, 2015 by Tyndale House Foundation. Used by permission of Tyndale House Publishers, Inc., Carol Stream, Illinois 60188. All rights reserved.

Scripture quotations marked (GNT) are from the Good News Translation in Today's English Version–Second Edition Copyright © 1992 by American Bible Society. Used by Permission. All rights reserved.

Preface

READERS OF THIS BOOK, who are approaching my material for the first time, may wish to know that some people who have read both of the original editions have informed me that, in some cases, *God's Address—Living with the Triune God: A Scripture Workbook* might perhaps turn out to be the easier introduction to things trinitarian than *The Lion, the Dove, & the Lamb*. And so, you are possibly holding the right book! It's ironic—but not atypical of God's ways—that the second book to be published should turn out to be in fact the one some folk ought to read ahead of the first book. I guess it depends upon how familiar any reader is with either the New Testament itself or some of the earlier centuries of church history. True; *The Lion, the Dove, & the Lamb* does necessarily contain some vital NT material assembled in chapters 4 and 5 before we go into the details of that early church history. These chapters were also deliberately kept to a basic level, showing how those early (Jewish) Christians struggled to interpret and articulate the gospel from the beginning. Either way, yet another approach might very well be to have both books and then mix-and-match them, copying-and-pasting chapters 4 and 5 after any reader(s) of *God's Address* has/have covered sessions 1–4. How to continue thereafter might depend upon how venturesome one is: either dive into those early centuries of the Christian church in *The Lion, the Dove, & the Lamb*, chapter 6 onwards; or stick with the more familiar territory of the NT. Although perhaps even if one does stick with this second course, one should be warned: the actual *way* sessions 5–9 of *God's Address* get presented, while covering seemingly familiar NT material well enough, might cause a number of surprises—I am given to understand. So be it! All in all; *Tolle! Lege!* "Take up and read!" Enjoy! And be blessed—and become a richer blessing in your practice of discipleship of the triune God, Father, Son, and Holy Spirit.

Acknowledgments

IN THE FIRST PLACE, I owe a debt of gratitude to those readers of *The Lion, the Dove, & the Lamb* who prompted the writing of this workbook. Without their desire to see how the biblical account of the economy of God's salvation might be "read" more fruitfully in a trinitarian vein, it would never have seen the light of day. In addition, thanks are due as before to the team of Wipf & Stock who produced this workbook. Their cheerful efficiency is most appreciated.

Countless others, too many to name—especially friends, parishioners, and colleagues—from diverse settings and even countries, have engaged in multiple ways with elements of the material of this workbook over the years. I'd like to think their responses and reactions, and especially their questions, have been well received and responded to by myself. Yet no doubt infelicities remain; and for these I alone am naturally responsible. And so, a heartfelt thanks to all these fellow pilgrims who have walked with me along God's Way in Christ Jesus, as we've turned—and turned again—and so begun to return to that Home wherein the triune God himself dwells in himself and yet also with his human creatures and they with God, Father, Son, and Holy Spirit, in holiness and truth, in grace and steadfast love. To such a God the greatest acknowledgement of all![1]

Christchurch, New Zealand
St. John of the Cross, 2016

1. Readers of *LDL* will hear echoes of Jean-Luc Marion's *In the Self's Place* and the poem it prompted, to be found at the conclusion of that earlier book of mine, 192–96.

Further Acknowledgments

I AM GRATEFUL TO those readers of both the first book of mine, *The Lion, the Dove, & the Lamb*, and this its subsequent follow-up, *God's Address—Living with the Triune God*, for their responses to what I wrote. In many cases, they have helped to improve the clarity of the ideas and so the texts themselves. They have pushed me also to include additional material, the extent of which prompted the possibility of these two revised editions. In particular, I am grateful to Ivor Davidson, Myk Habets and Paul Henderson, whose encouragement tipped the balance in favor of presenting the revisions to Wipf & Stock for publishing. And so lastly, I acknowledge again the staff of Wipf & Stock for their intricate handling of all the revisions: a huge "Thank-you" to them all.

Abbreviations

ABD	Freedman, David Noel, ed. *The Anchor Bible Dictionary*. 6 Vols. New York: Doubleday, 1992.
ANF	*Ante-Nicene Fathers*, reprinted Grand Rapids, Eerdmans, 1987.
CD	Barth, Karl. *Church Dogmatics*. 4 vols. Edited by G. W. Bromiley and T. F. Torrance. Edinburgh: T&T Clark, 1956–75.
EVV	The various English versions of the Bible.
LDL	Black, A. Bryden. *The Lion, the Dove, & the Lamb: An Exploration into the Nature of the Christian God as Trinity*. Eugene, OR: Wipf & Stock, rev. ed. 2018.
ST	Jenson, Robert W. *Systematic Theology*. 2 vols. New York: Oxford University Press, 1997/99.

Introduction

IT IS ONE THING to attempt to write formal Christian theology—albeit in a way that is hopefully digestible by "ordinary Christians." It is perhaps quite another to thereafter provide for these Christians practical resources that may more readily assist them to grow into what Jesus, the Lord of the church, both offers and calls the people of God toward. Just so, firstly, an essay of mine, *The Lion, the Dove, & the Lamb: An Exploration into the Nature of the Christian God as Trinity* (henceforth *LDL*), which was first published in 2015 by Wipf & Stock. Although this book explicitly gave readers a number of questions for reflection after each chapter, endeavoring to help them engage further with the material, the overall tenor of the text was to tell a particular story of the Trinity. What precipitated this way of speaking and understanding of God? How did it subsequently develop and why? What were some of the consequences? And finally, how might we tie it all together more systematically? And all this by means of a model of the triune God derived from the very embodiment of this God's mission in the midst of human history. While there were clear pointers along the way of how all this concretely impacts—or could impact—the ordinary lives of Christians, some readers of *LDL* believed that, in the end, a fuller biblical resource might assist them with their discipleship of Jesus in a specifically trinitarian vein. Hence now this workbook.

This workbook, however, is not merely yet another scriptural study. Two things are paramount. First, given the central axiom of all recent studies, which seek to revive the doctrine of the Trinity, to be that everything the triune God *does* in the economy of salvation properly expresses who God *is* as Trinity,[1] the major focus of these studies is the economy itself, as witnessed to in the Bible. But what is meant, exactly, by this short-hand term, "the economy" of salvation? *LDL*, page 53, note 4, says this:

> This expression, "the economy," became an important piece of shorthand [in the early church], first employed by Ignatius of Antioch in his Letter to the Ephesians (20). It's also helpful and important to see its etymology. *Oikos* is Greek for household, *oikonomia* then becoming the administration of that household, notably through its *oikonomos* or steward. See especially Ephesians 1–3, where a whole lot of words, both nouns and verbs (to build), use this *oiko*-root [and so see session 6 below, which unpacks all these ideas clearly].

So the question then becomes: Who is this God who has so acted in the economy of salvation, executing this plan and carrying it out through the history of those specific events attested in the pages of Christian Scripture? As *LDL* made plain, the answer is the God and Father of the Lord Jesus Christ—bearing in mind "Christ" means the anointed one, the Messiah of Israel, the One on whom the Holy Spirit descended and remained, and who subsequently shared that self-same Holy Spirit with his followers in the church, John 1:32–33; Acts 2:33 (see *LDL*, chapters 4 and 5). Just so, "God" equals Father, Son, and Holy Spirit.

Second, we need to note the manner in which this extensive Bible study will be undertaken; we can approach studying the Scriptures in a number of ways. Here we shall be employing a most traditional term from the recesses of our church traditions. For here, I believe, we might find resources that may be freshened up and reminted for our day, and which may uniquely address the plight we appear to be in regarding our present "reading" of the

---

1. Rahner famously expresses it like this: "the economic Trinity is the immanent Trinity and the immanent Trinity is the economic Trinity" (Rahner, *Trinity*, 22); or, the God who acts beyond or outside himself is truly as God is in himself as Trinity. See *LDL*, page 70, note 43, for the context and the qualification of this *Grundaxiom* of Rahner's.

INTRODUCTION

Holy Scriptures. While the word "manuduction" appears weird to our contemporary ears, a simple exercise in etymology gives us the meaning: *manus* is Latin for "hand," and *ducere* means "to lead." The approach is borrowed from the world of medieval Christianity as portrayed by Peter Candler Jr. in his *Theology, Rhetoric, Manuduction, or Reading Scripture Together on the Path to God*. That is, I am presenting a particular reading strategy in this workbook.

I wish to take the reader(s) by the hand and lead them along a specific path in relation to Scripture. As a narrator of Holy Scripture, I will "lead by the hand" the reader(s) using the various sessions laid out here, viewed as an "itinerary" of the Way of Christ, of Jesus Christ as the Way or *Via* to life with/in the triune God. Candler writes in his chapter 2, entitled "Itineraries; or, Theology as Manuduction," that the "route to *salus* [which is Latin for "salvation"] is not *contained* by the text, but, as it were, furnished by it."[2] The result is that "the itinerary of the soul is the function of a pedagogy of manuduction [a specific teaching method], by which the reader is not merely given information but led into God"[3] as they pursue the exercise of reading along with the scriptural text offered here. As applied to this workbook, then, I too am not concerned merely to convey information. Rather, I wish to furnish for readers a specific manner of "reading" the text of Scripture, by offering a series of particular Scripture studies. By means of these studies, we shall be meeting with Jesus at every turn, and in such a way that *he* now takes us by the hand and leads us into the very Life of God, that Life he came to introduce us to. Just so **1 John 1:1–4**, with its specific trinitarian emphasis.[4]

And so, let us embark upon this journey of "reading" the Holy Scriptures in a particular Way, a Way that leads to nothing less than a New Life immersed in the love and freedom of the Living

---

2. Candler, *Theology, Rhetoric, Manuduction*, 45, emphasis original.

3. Ibid., 44.

4. It is significant that 1 John starts by echoing the language of "witness" found in John 15:26–27. The authority of the letter derives from the Holy Spirit himself enveloping the human testimony of those who were "with Jesus from the beginning."

God, Father, Son, and Holy Spirit. Here we present a particular itinerary, of following along the given Way this specific God has come among us, as narrated in the Holy Scriptures, of following after Jesus Christ, to whom all Scripture directs us. For the church may duly recognise these Scriptures as both the singular witness to and the unique instrument in the saving economy of the triune God, and so as "the divinely appointed servant" (after John Webster)[5] of this economy. Everything depends upon our grasping as fully as possible this economy of grace—or rather, of being graciously grasped more fully by this triune God (Phil 3), whose identity is declared in his economy. And so, it is to the story of this economy of salvation and the means of our participation within it that we now turn—which very means is itself derived from a specific pattern or form of New Testament (NT) teaching that is also a form of life, as we shall see. For Jesus desires to "lead us by the hand" through his biblical word to the "place" where he stays (abides/dwells; see **John 1:38–39**. Also see John 1:1, 18, and 13–17 especially, where "abide" is often and typically found).

A note on how to proceed. Those **Bible texts written in bold** are to be specifically read. While it does not matter too much which translation is followed, if the workbook is being used in a group setting (see Notes for Leaders in the appendix), then perhaps various different translations might be brought by different participants with benefit. Also, these readings are better read aloud in a group, and any others pursued subsequently at leisure. Where passages are printed in full, translations used are noted (although sometimes modified). Footnotes mostly suggest resources for further study, and

---

5. Webster, *Holy Scripture*, 30–31. "Where sanctification indicates the dogmatic ontology of the text as the servant of the divine self-communicative presence." Webster uses the category of "sanctification," applied to Holy Scripture, as the means of acknowledging its due role in the triune God's economy of saving grace. See his chapters 1 and 2. Swain, *Trinity, Revelation, and Reading* also offers a wonderful appraisal of how we may learn to "read" Holy Scripture, given its nature and purpose. For, to paraphrase, it serves as the necessary literary instrument communicating across time and space God's desire for covenantal communion among humans achieving the fullness of the divine glory (e.g. 2 Cor 3–4, 1 Jn 1:1–4).

INTRODUCTION

may be pursued as much or as little as any reader(s) might see fit. A bibliography is provided at the back of the workbook.

A note on the title, *God's address—Living with the Triune God*. With typical double entendre, the word "address" means a number of things. The entire economy of salvation shows the God who speaks, and acts, and who thereby addresses humanity. Scripture furthermore, by uniquely witnessing to this address, continues to enact this divine word among humans. The title also catches the epigraph, John 1:38–39, and the place where Jesus is staying/lodging. Yet finally, properly, the Son's "location" or "space" is his being ever turned toward the Father's "heart"/"bosom" (John 1:18), depicting an intense intimacy between them. All these ideas are captured by the title, and convey humanity's own eventual due "address," given the Father's sending the Son and the Holy Spirit into the world. For humanity's destiny is nothing less than living with the triune God at God's own "address."[6]

---

6. An alternative working title of this workbook at one point was *Farther Up and Farther In: The Full Story of Christian Initiation into the Life of the Triune God*. It is derived from C. S. Lewis's *The Last Battle*, where the children and all the redeemed creatures enter at the end into the fullness of the Garden's life, where the inside is greater and more spacious than the outside. Such, too, is the true life of Christians as they begin to enter into and share in nothing less than the divine nature, the life of the triune God—albeit in the eschatological manner of God's own Way of salvation via Jesus and the Holy Spirit. In these days of snappy titles, it was replaced! For all that, either title tries to do justice to Jesus' leading readers of Scripture home to his Father and our Father, his God and our God (John 20:17). (See Lewis, *Last Battle*, 158–65.)

Part One (Session 1)

The Story Unfolds

Abraham to Exile

The Gospel accounts of Jesus vary, with Mark, probably the first written version, beginning with the ministry of John the Baptist, who immediately prepares Jesus' Way, locating that Way within the prophetic narratives of Isaiah and Malachi (Mal 3:1, plus Exod 23:20, and Isa 40:3). Matthew and Luke begin further back, with the birth of Jesus, their respective accounts having different emphases. Matthew, for example, presents Jesus' genealogical identity as the rich climax—indeed, a new beginning—of the Abraham and David stories, and Luke the resumption of the Spirit of prophecy in various guises. Then John's Gospel goes all the way back to "in the beginning was the Word." For the person of Jesus is to be located uniquely within the God of Genesis's very own identity, the Creator of all the earth, as well as the human matrix of Israel, and Mary and Joseph. We, however, begin this workbook with the adult Jesus and the ministry of John in the wilderness, only then to return all the way back to Israel's origins.

Reading—Matt 3:1-12

What exactly is it that John the Baptist is expecting?

Part One (Session 1): The Story Unfolds

What is it about the Jewish faith that instills this sense of expectation?

To answer these questions, we return to the beginning of Israel's story.

The story of God's dealings with people takes on specific focus with the call of Abram/Abraham, the ancestor of the Israelite nation. Previously in Gen 1–11 the scope has been global, even cosmic, with God's relationship with the entire creation to the fore, and then with humanity itself generally.

Gen 12:1–3 God promises three things to Abram—land, descendants, blessing

The entire Old Testament (OT) story circles around these three: *Will* there be descendants? Will they live in the land—or not? Will they be *blessed* there—or not? will *they be* a blessing? Or will the land "vomit them out" (Leviticus)? Will a remnant then return, perhaps? A raft of such permutations drives the story, while it looks again and again as if God's promise, and Abraham's line, is in jeopardy. Yet both keep being renewed, in various ways, as an ongoing testament to God's faithfulness and purpose.

Gen 15:1–6 (–21) The covenant between Yahweh and Abram
Gen 17:1–8 (–16) The covenant renewed (Abraham and Sarah's names changed: inserting the H implies God's *ruach* (Spirit) will now enliven each of them to "make" a son)
Gen 22:(1–) 15–18 The promise repeated

It is this covenant promise that gives the Israelites a keen sense of *history*. They have a *destiny*, since they have a *destination*, a goal, which God has promised them and toward which he is leading them. The nature of this goal becomes more apparent as time goes on, as God guides his people.[1]

---

1. Readers who wish to pursue the significance of these summary opening paragraphs might go to Clines, *Theme of the Pentateuch*.

The patriarchal age, depicted in the stories of Abraham and his descendants, envisages a world around 2000 to 1800 BC, in which God calls out a particular family.[2] The Exodus under Moses, set between say 1450 and 1290 BC, shows that family becoming a nation, and assuming the identity of God's particular and chosen people. (Read **Exod 1:1–14, chapter 3, 7:1–7, 12:1–20, 13:1–16, 15:1–21, the highlights of chapters 19–24 [19:1–6, 20:1–17, 24:1–11], chapters 32–34**, and 40:33–38). The beginning of the Ten Commandments encapsulates the Exodus narrative: "I am Yahweh your God, who brought you out of Egypt, out of the land of slavery. You shall have no other gods before me" (Exod 20:2–3). Deuteronomy sees Israel poised to enter the promised land and fulfill God's promise to Abraham and Moses, living there as a particular people, covenanted with Yahweh, and demonstrating "righteousness and justice" among themselves (**Deut 7:6–11, 6:1–9**). While the conquest and initial settlement of Canaan occurs under Joshua, the period of "the Judges" is seen to be somewhat problematic, with unsettlement as much as settlement existing side by side: conflict, death, rape, murder, and horror mix with elements of peace, order, justice, and true worship. Round and round we go until **Judg 21:25** is the lamentable conclusion. Just so finally, the call for a king (1 Samuel), a leader, who as much as anything else can fix the Philistine problem once and for all. Initially, Saul reigned c. 1020–1010, and then David c. 1010–970, with Solomon succeeding him until c. 930. The Davidic–Solomonic era is seen as a golden age in Israelite history.[3] (See especially **1 Kgs 4:20–25**, which takes up the language of the Genesis passages, and **Pss 2** and **72**, which themselves reflect Nathan's prophetic oracle on the Davidic dynasty, 2 Sam 7.) Following Solomon's death, the nation was divided into two groups, the northern and southern kingdoms, with the promises of God once more seemingly exposed to threat.

2. The key words here are "depicted" and "envisages." See Hendel, *Remembering Abraham*, esp. chapters 2 and 3, "Remembering Abraham" and "Historical Memories in the Patriarchal Narratives," 31–43, 45–55.

3. As with the figure of Abraham, so with David, but now in a different key, given David's central place in OT Scripture—not least regarding David's "greater son." See Brueggemann, *David's Truth*.

PART ONE (SESSION 1): THE STORY UNFOLDS

By 740 BC (the year in which Isaiah had his vision, **chapter 6**, and the year Uzziah, king of Southern Judah, died) the story reached a climactic turning point with the rise and expansion of Assyrian power under Tiglath-Pileser III. His successor, Shalmaneser V, sacked Samaria, capital of the Northern Kingdom, in 722, ushering in religious and political turmoil and uncertainty. Hezekiah became king of Judah in 715 and tried to reform the faith amidst much aggression from Assyria. Jerusalem was itself besieged by Sennacherib in 701 but was spared, even as the surrounding district was pillaged. God's involvement is recorded in Isaiah. **Read only 2:1–5, 6–22, and 10:5—11:9**. God *is* to have his day, when he will enact his judgment-and-salvation over a fallen, broken, rebellious world—despite the apparent odds.

The seventh century BC was a messy, confusing time for Judah. Things again came to a head after Josiah's reforms (640–609) failed to stem the tide of apostasy. The year 605 saw the convincing rise to power of Babylon under Nebuchadnezzar as a result of Egypt's total defeat at the battle of Carchemish (2 Kgs 24:7; Jer 46). Inevitably, Judah and Jerusalem got caught up in all this! The city was occupied in March 597, with Nebuchadnezzar deporting the leaders of the nation to Babylon. A stupid uprising under Zedekiah, who was the appointed governor left in charge by the Babylonians, caused the destruction of the temple and city walls in 587–586, when the majority of the people were also taken into exile.

Summary Conclusion

There's little doubt the period of exile was a fiery crucible for the people of Israel and their faith. It's also most probable many of her now extant writings were explicitly gathered together during this period (and afterwards), and used to rally these people who were now wrested from their homeland, to grant them a sense of identity despite such a catastrophic loss.

This session has plotted an elementary outline of this story, from ancestors to exile, from origins to . . . well, what? Our next session pursues a form of an answer. But instead of chronicling an account along a timeline, with the people of Israel's rise and fall, it will assemble more systematically a number of key motifs of Israel's religious worldview, grounding them in some basic religious practices. For the OT offers us both history and theology all combined together.[4] By separating them out more distinctly in these first two sessions, we may then become better equipped to gauge how God's purposes in the economy of salvation come to fruition in the Story of Jesus—the topic of Part Two, Session 3.

---

4. Proposed reconstructions of "Israelite history" continue unabated, since the very history of historiography itself (both modern linear-critical history and a return to "participatory history"), as applied to the Bible's body of literature, is a constant focus of scholarly attention. Similarly, "Theologies of the Old Testament" abound. See for example Hasel, *OT Theology*, who brilliantly sets the scene, with subsequent offerings by the likes of Rolf Knierim, Walter Brueggemann, Paul House, Bruce Waltke, Walter Moberly, and John Goldingay.

Part One (Session 2)

Get Ready!

The Day of Yahweh

But still, God did not leave matters there—*Israel's Future Hope*:

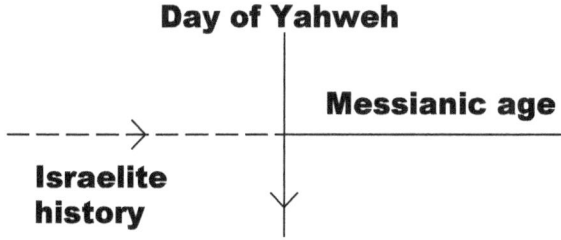

Figure 1: Israel's Future Hope

Up ahead, on the horizon of history, is this Great Happening, the Day of the Lord, when the God of Israel will declare and show himself to be God indeed, the Creator of all the earth and everything in it, and the ruler of all history and every people—and notably Israel. [We leave aside the development of this lynch-pin idea, the Day of Yahweh, from, for example, Amos 5 to Zechariah's closing oracles, despite its fascination. We also do not go into how later Jewish apocalyptic literature devised wondrous schemes associated with this unveiling of God's sovereign purposes and eventual glory.]

God's Address—Living with the Triune God

Major Motifs Associated with the Day of Yahweh/the Lord

▶ *Davidic King.* The following are some major references. **2 Sam 7:1-29**. **Micah's** three sections, each beginning with "Listen!" [**1:2, 3:1, 6:1**], all include, under themes of hope after judgment, *shepherding* (**2:12, 4:8, 5:4 [5:1-5]** and **7:14**), the "shepherd" being a basic image of kingship in the OT. **Isa 1-12** is rich with royal imagery, focussed on Mt. Zion, David's City (**2:1-5, 5:1-7, 9:1-7, 10:33—11:9**). **Isa 55** concludes by referring to David, vv. 3-4. **Jer 23:1-6** and **Ezek 34:1-24** contrast present bad kings with the Future Good King; **Ezek 17** has a parable and its interpretation of monarchial restoration after judgment. Many throughout the church's history have read the **Psalms** as if the Messiah, and so Jesus, might be referenced through many a text. But while it is easy enough to see key Psalms cited in the NT (e.g., Pss 110, 118, 16), we shall not attempt here to examine this notion in any detail.[1] Rather, we need to note how *the seams of the Psalter*, with their Davidic theme, editorially arrange the five books: **Ps 2** opens Book 1, while **Ps 72** closes Book 2, and **Ps 89** (reference 2 Sam 7) closes Book 3, with its apparent failure answered by Book 4's **Pss 93** and **95-100**: Yahweh himself reigns indeed! **Ps 132** underscores the links between Zion/Jerusalem and monarchy and Yahweh's purposes. A final Davidic Psalm of praise, **145**, heads the concluding Psalms of praise, **146-150**, all of which together close the Psalter in a deliberate crescendo. Lastly, note **Zech 9-14**, a complex set of oracles, which includes **9:9-10, 11:4-17**,

---

1. Sanders, *Triune God*, chapter 8, "Old Covenant Adumbration," delightfully shows how the early church fathers readily identified Jesus, the anointed messiah, throughout the Psalms: sections "Retrospective Prosoponic Identification" and "Prosoponic Exegesis of the Psalms," 226-37 (where the word "prosoponic" simply refers to a reading technique that seeks to identify the speaker(s) involved in any OT passage, *prosōpon* meaning "face"). His concluding section, "Rereading the Psalms as Trinitarian Praise," becomes the due climax.

PART ONE (SESSION 2): GET READY!

12:7—13:1, and 13:7-9, and all of which associate royal Davidic themes amidst universal judgment-and-salvation.

- *New Covenant.* **Jer 31:31-34** and **Ezek 36:24-28**.
- *Holy Spirit.* There are too many references to specify, but on account of the Rabbis speaking of the Lord's "shekinah glory," note **Ezek 1, 3:12-15, chapter 11,** and **37:1-14**. And see too **Joel chapter 2**'s plague of locusts, leading into the famous verses **28-32**. See too **Isa 63:7-14** and **Hag 2:2-9**.
- *Servant figure.* **Isa 42:1-7, 49:1-6, 50:4-9, 52:13—53:12, 61:1-3** will be taken up specifically later.
- *Son of man figure.* **Dan 7:9-14**, which will also be taken up directly by Jesus (see Mark).
- *National restoration.* Again, too frequent to specify, but see, for example, **Amos 9:11-15**. Notably, Isaiah, Ezekiel, and others view such restoration as a *New Exodus*, Isa 35:8, 40:3-8, 51:9-11, 52:11-12, 63:11-14; Ezek 20:33-42, 36:24-28.
- *Individual resurrection.* **Ps 16:9-11; Isa 26:19, 53:11** (see modern EVV translations only, following the Dead Sea Scrolls); **Dan 12:2-3**.
- From all of which may be concluded that *"Yahweh is there"* (**Ezek 48:35**. See also Ezek 37:24-28).

God is Present Among His People

To better appreciate this vital conclusion,[2] we might take a brief tour through the matrix of Israelite religion in the OT via its origins in the "cult." This is a difficult word for us modern people, because its reality is so alien to our contemporary world. To its world belong the ideas of daily sacrifices to the gods, sacred/profane (rites, places, and people), clean/unclean (or pure/impure, again, people and things especially), acceptable gift/abomination,

---

2. Beale, *Temple and the Church's Mission*, has a detailed picture of this key biblical motif.

shrines, high places, sanctuaries, altars, fire, and blood. All the paraphernalia (and gore perhaps to us!) of the ancient ways of worship is the cradle of OT worship.

The *object* of all this is *to enter the presence of God*. First and foremost in the OT, God is a *Presence* to be sought and experienced at a sanctuary in an act of worship. "To seek God's face" is the technical term. The cult was designed to bring about this very thing. See, for example, **Pss 24:3-6, 27:7-9**, and **105:3-4**. This last Psalm reference is notable, since Augustine cites it frequently in his *De Trinitate* as we saw in *LDL*, page 92.

1. *Modes of God's presence*

    a. Face: **Pss 95:2, 114:7, 16:11; Isa 64:1-8; Deut 31:16-18**.

    b. Name: **Deut 12:5, 11, 26:1-2; 1 Kgs 8:16-20, 27, 29**.

    c. Temple: See previous verses, especially **1 Kgs 8:22-53; 2 Chr 5:7-14; Ezek 10, 11:22-23; Mal 3:1**.

    d. Zion/Jerusalem: **Pss 9:11, 48:1-2, 74:1-2, 76:1-2** and many others. **Isa 2:1-5, 4:2-6, 8:18, 40:9**.

    e. Glory: **Exod 24:15-18, 40:34-38; 1 Kgs 8:10-11; Ezek 43:1-5**.

    f. Tent: **Exod 25-40** (the design plans for the tabernacle, and their execution), especially **Exod 29:43-46; 1 Chr 16:1**.

    g. Ark: **Pss 80:1, 99:1; 1 Chr 13:6; Jer 3:15-17**.

2. *Means of access into this presence*

    Let us begin with **Exod 19:10-22**. Following our exclusion from Eden, humanity cannot readily walk with the Creator. But God's purpose for us is full and free fellowship with himself. This may only be achieved at *great and elaborate cost*. Thus, Leviticus follows Exod 25-40, and we are introduced to the roles of *sacrifice* and *priest* in Lev 1-7 and 8-9, respectively.

PART ONE (SESSION 2): GET READY!

3. *Results of worship*

True worship is not mere attendance at the sanctuary. First, coming into the presence of God is a happening of great joy and delight. It is a celebration, a festive occasion. Again and again this is stressed in the OT. See, for example, **Ps 100**! It is not insignificant that the last sacrifice mentioned in the Leviticus list deals with the peace or fellowship offering. (See also **Exod 24:9–11**.)

Second, authentic worship overflows into everyday life. The task of the priest, even in OT times, was to give instruction (*torah*) on how to live, as well as to offer sacrifices. Moreover, there was a special group of cult prophets at the sanctuary, whose job it was to mediate the divine will. **Amos 5** and **Isa 58** are good examples of prophetic teaching on worship.

One last comment. One of the key elements of Israel's future hope in the end times is expressed in terms of Mt. Zion and God's sanctuary at Jerusalem, where he would emphatically come to dwell with his people—Isa 2:1–4, 4:4–6, 11:9, chapter 12, and **Ezek 48:35** again (see Heb 12:18–24 and Rev 21–22 for its NT fulfillment).

How all these motifs play out in detail in the period from the restoration under the Persian king Cyrus, 539 BC, through Ezra and Nehemiah (mid-fifth century), the invasion of Alexander the Great (332–323 BC) and the resulting dominance of Hellenistic culture, and on down to the Maccabean revolts (167–142), and then finally the Romans, need not concern us here. Suffice to say, Jewry is kept waiting . . .

And John the Baptist comes preaching in the desert of Judea, **Matt 3:1–12** (Mal 3:1–4, 4:1–3)

God's Day is about to dawn!
You can see the Sun's rays breaking over the *immediate* horizon!
Watch out! Get ready!

Questions for Reflection

1. Do you have *a sense of destiny* to your life, to what degree, and how does it affect you?
2. How might all this talk of OT history and *God in this history* impact upon your *own* history?
3. What do you *expect* from the *God who promises*?
4. Combining questions 1–3 now, the Bible witnesses to the warp and woof of God's Covenant History with his people.[3] Covenants are broadly of two kinds, conditional ones and unconditional ones, and the OT inscribes both. The former suggests full mutuality between the parties, with consequences, obligations, and responsibilities for each, while the latter stresses the free initiative of the one party to establish and maintain the covenant relationship. How might we juggle the tension between these two types? And what impact does this tension have upon your own individual life's story or history? See the final Session for the resolution of this tension in the ministry of Jesus as Paul interprets it in Galatians. And see too "A Covenant Summary," pages 75–83.
5. This final reflection raises the stakes but is well worth pondering. We take our cue from a man called Auerbach, who is contrasting the likes of Homer's *Odyssey* and Old Testament narrative:

   > Far from seeking, like Homer, merely to make us forget our own reality for a few hours, the OT seeks to overcome our reality: we are to fit our own life into its world, feel ourselves to be elements in its structure of universal history . . . into it everything that is known about the world must be fitted as an ingredient of the divine plan.

---

3. The literature on the idea of "covenant" is vast, due to both its use in the long history of theology and OT scholarship over recent decades. A popular introduction is Rhodes, *Covenants Made Simple*. A more studious option is Horton, *Covenant Theology*. A classic scholarly overview is Hillers, *Covenant*, and more fully, Kline, *Structure*.

PART ONE (SESSION 2): GET READY!

What might it mean for your own life's story to be fitted into such a bold and broad story line as that offered in the whole OT—the whole Bible even? Imagine what it might be like to envisage your own life caught up into this grand biblical drama, or theodrama even.[4]

---

4. Readers who wish to pursue further the idea of the Bible's being a Grand Story or Drama might go to Bauckham, "Reading Scripture as a Coherent Story."

Part Two (Session 3)

Ready for What? For Whom?

Jesus' Coming

But things did not turn out quite as the Baptist expected. Nor was he alone in his puzzlement. Not only were "the authorities" frequently at odds with Jesus, even the poor disciples didn't get it (e.g., Mark 8:17-21). In the first place, see **Matt 3:13-17** (the voice from heaven echoes **Ps 2:7, Isa 42:1,** and **Gen 22:2, 12, 16**).[1] Then, and crucially, we have **Matt 11:2-15**. Verse 6 of Matt 11 is surely one of the key texts of the entire NT: "Blessed is the one who does not take offense at me"—literally, is not *scandalized* in me, is not scandalized at the *way* God is fulfilling his OT promises through me and with me and in me, Jesus. For the point is this: "Now when John heard in prison about the deeds of the Messiah, he sent word by his disciples and said to him, 'Are you the one who is to come, or shall we look for another?'" (Matt 11:2-3, ESV). John's message betrays bafflement, and little wonder, for one of the deeds Messiah was to do was "to free captives from prison"—or so Isaiah 42:7 and 61:1 seem to promise! And John's identity is necessarily caught up with Jesus' identity. For if Jesus is *not* the One Who is to Come, then neither is John the One to Prepare his Way.

---

1. Significantly Matt 3:16 softens Mark's heavens "being rent apart" (1:10), which cites Isa 64:1, evoking further that Yahweh is now decisively on the move—"watch out! get ready!"

PART TWO (SESSION 3): READY FOR WHAT? FOR WHOM?

What's up here? In brief, the Baptizer, expected by John the Baptist, is *himself* to become the Baptized One, i.e., the Judge (of the Day of Yahweh) is to become the Judged One.[2] See **Luke 12:49-50** and **Mark 10:35-45** (Isa 51:17-23 regarding the "cup" is also found in Mark 14:36; and "give his life a ransom for many" probably references Isa 53, notably vv. 10-12).

Only when Jesus has first become "the Lamb of God," submitting himself to the divine baptismal judgment (John 1:29), does he, can he, then become "life giving Spirit" (1 Cor 15:45), the promised One "who baptizes with Holy Spirit" (John 1:33). See especially Acts 2:32-39 (more of this later).

John 1:29-34 is a good summary, clearly revealing Jesus' *double* identity at the beginning and the end of John's "testimony," with its content in between fleshing this twin identity out. See **John 7:37-39** as well, for only when Jesus is "glorified"—which in the Fourth Gospel means when he is "lifted up" in *both* crucifixion *and* resurrection—does/can the Spirit come. Nor should we miss the fact that these events at the Jordan anticipate, prefigure even, the climax of Jesus' mission. On the one hand, Jesus' identification with John's baptism of repentance for sin begins the journey that will climax in his being the Lamb of God at Golgotha, and so Yahweh's Suffering Servant. Then, on the other hand, the combined voice of Ps 2 and Gen 22 at the baptism is proleptic, anticipating the reality of Easter Day and Jesus being "declared Son of God in power according to the Spirit of holiness through resurrection of the dead" (Rom 1:4, also see Acts 2:36).

Another creedal summary is found at **1 Cor 15:3-5**, which complements well John 1:29-34.

Picking up that key OT motif of divine Presence, John's Gospel is especially succinct: "the Word became flesh and dwelt (literally, *tabernacled*) among us, and we saw his *glory*" (**John 1:1, 14, 18, 2:18-22**).[3] Jesus is now the Meeting Place between God and

---

2. This last expression echoes the title of the subsection 59.2, "The Judge Judged in our Place," from Barth's *CD IV/1*, 211-83.

3. See especially Perrin, *Jesus the Temple*. Perrin suggests this appreciation of Jesus' identity may be traced back to Jesus himself. Moreover, it acts as the basis of a counter-temple movement that has numerous consequences (e.g., session 6), which both fulfills the OT and yet also radically transforms it (see

humans—the New Tabernacle, the New Temple, the *locale* of the entire cult. The OT modes of God's presence, and the means of access into that presence, all coalesce in Jesus, response to whom in worship and service (Rom 12:1) prompts joy and the obedience of faith (so e.g. Luke/Acts and Rom 1:5, 16:26). (The Letter to the Hebrews will of course absolutely go to town at this point!)

See too **Matt 1:23, 12:6, 18:20, 28:20**.

Summary Conclusion[4]

The Son of God, sent by the Father in the power of the Holy Spirit, has become a human being, Jesus of Nazareth. "Born of a woman, born under the Law" (Gal 4:4), "in the likeness of sinful flesh" (Rom 8:3), Jesus is our substitute (the one who takes the place of an injured player—the Fall) and our representative (the captain, who stands for the whole team). In and through him God brings about his kingdom/establishes his sovereign rule, by taking his wrath "against all that is proud and lofty, all that is exalted" (Isa 2:12) into/upon himself and recreating humanity in a radically new way. The cross and resurrection/ascension are the climax of God's purposes in and with Jesus (apart from the Second Coming and all that). Read **2 Cor 5:17** and **Gal 6:15**, as well as **Gal 3:13-14** and **4:4-6**. Our final session will take up Gal 3-4 more fully.

In other words, the Day of the Lord has broken into the *middle* of human history in the course of the career of one person, Jesus, God's Anointed.[5] See especially **John 11:17-27**, the story of

---

"A basic analogy" in Questions for Reflection below).

4. Systematic theology has traditionally summarized the ministry of Jesus through the notion of the *manus triplex Christi*, the threefold offices of prophet, priest, and king, those three key OT institutions that Jesus supremely fulfills. The prophetic sees Jesus herald the Gospel, witnessing to God's revelation of grace and truth. The priestly sees Jesus as the mediator of reconciliation and redemption, vitally through the cross. The kingly endows Jesus with divine authority as the reinstituted "royal man."

5. Wright, *Resurrection*, provides a comprehensive examination of this way of expressing the issue. For the mission and ministry of Jesus generally, see Wright, *Jesus and Victory*. For a delightfully rich reading of the Gospels as "a catalytic

PART TWO (SESSION 3): READY FOR WHAT? FOR WHOM?

Lazarus. This Day of Yahweh/the Lord is not only an event now, but is supremely a *Person*—"I am the Resurrection and the Life." While Martha's answer to Jesus repeats sound Jewish theological expectations (v. 24), in point of fact the Day of Yahweh (recall Exod 3:14) is standing four feet from her, speaking with her![6] Nor does her formal confession (v. 27, using rich Johannine vocabulary) seem truly perceptive, in the light of her subsequent retort (v. 39). Only the final "sign" itself—Lazarus's return to life—speaks for itself: Jesus is indeed the One he claims to be!

A pair of diagrams will help explain this chronological shift:

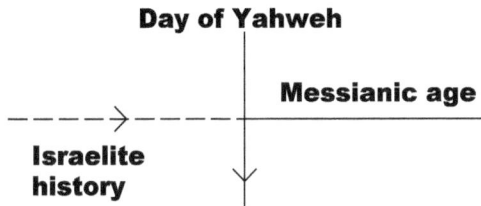

Figure 2: Israel's Future Hope (once more)

---

fusion of Israel's Scripture and the story of Jesus," see Hays, *Reading Backwards*, and more fulsomely, *Echoes*. The latter offers us a profound presentation of "divine identity Christology" via all four Gospels, with their respective narrative renderings depicting Jesus through the lens of the Hebrew Scriptures as "the embodiment of the divine presence in the world." And last but by no means least, Hurtado, *One God, One Lord*, now helpfully summarizes the NT scholarly debate of the evidence of viewing Jesus as being on a par with Yahweh—the practice of which emerged essentially very early (the central claim of chapters 3, 4, and 5 of *LDL*)—in his Epilogue to the third edition, 135–88.

6. See Köstenberger and Swain, *Father, Son and Spirit*, for a good examination of the Fourth Gospel's Trinitarian theology (and pages 121–26 regarding the "I am" sayings). To view Trinitarian theology via the key motif of the Tetragrammaton (YHWH) and Jesus as the bearer of this divine Name, see Soulen, *The Divine Name(s)*.

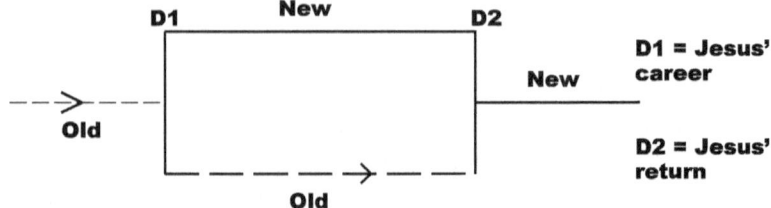

Figure 3: The Christian Fulfilment

The Day of Yahweh has indeed arrived, but in the Person of Jesus and his completed mission, in whom "new creation" has begun. For the rest, the Old Age of sin and death continues—even as there *are* due "signs" of the New Age continually breaking into the present, in faith, hope, and love, notably in the church's mission to and for the world. Only at the Second Coming, the Parousia, will all this be finally done away with—see **1 Cor 15:20-28** and **Rev 21-22**. The next session will take this up again in greater detail—especially how it is that Christians live concurrently between both Old and New Ages, as they participate in extending the rule of the now exalted Son of Man over the nations of this world (Matt 28:16-20; Dan 7:14, 18), by reflecting the Servant of Yahweh's "light" among "all the nations" (see Isa 42:6, 49:6, 2:2-4; Matt 5:16, 4:12-16; Luke 2:25-32 and 36-38, 3:6, 24:46-47; Acts 13:47, 28:28; Isa 40:1, 5, 52:9-10).

PART TWO (SESSION 3): READY FOR WHAT? FOR WHOM?

Questions for Reflection

6. How does the example of John the Baptist govern the *way* we expect God to deliver on his promises?

7. And how might we cultivate this sense of *expectation* on the one hand and of *waiting to discern* God's actual ways with the world on the other?

8. And *now* how does all this talk of *God in history* impact upon your sense of your *own* life's history and how you might fit into God's own Story—one which is implacably now the Story of God-and-humanity in Christ Jesus? Most helpful in answering such questions is Bartholomew and Goheen, *Drama of Scripture*.

9. *A basic analogy.* The OT presents us with a whole lot of pieces of a jigsaw puzzle from a box. These pieces consist of *people* (like Abraham, Isaac, Jacob, Moses, Joshua, David), *events* (like the exodus, exile, and restoration), *institutions* (like priesthood, temple, its cult and sacrifices, prophecy, kingship), and essential cultural *traits* (like Torah, covenant, creation theology, Wisdom), plus those *motifs* from the first studies above not already mentioned. The trick is then to see Jesus and his mission in the NT as providing *the picture on the lid* that fits them all together, fulfilling them—even if in rather unexpected, even radical ways! Capturing this idea of the completed "picture on the lid," Origen fondly describes Jesus in an extraordinarily compressed formulation of his identity as αὐτοβασιλεία (*autobasileia*). We may translate this as "the kingdom itself in person."[7]

---

7. Two examples of this fond expression. Origen says this of the parable of the unforgiving servant, Matt 18:23–35: "But if it be likened to such a king, and one who has done such things, who must we say that it is but the Son of God? For He is the King of the heavens, and as He is absolute Wisdom and absolute Righteousness and absolute Truth, is He not so also *absolute Kingdom*? [αὐτοβασιλεία] . . . But if you enquire into the meaning of the words, 'Theirs is the kingdom of heaven,' you may say that Christ is theirs in so far as He is *absolute Kingdom* [αὐτοβασιλεία]." Origen, "Matthew," in *ANF IX*, 498. Or see now *Spirit and Fire*, 362: "The Son of God is king of heaven. And just

We simply cannot understand the NT without the Old, yet the OT itself only comes into its own in the light of the New. St Augustine's famous saying is apt: "The New Testament is hidden [Latin: *latet*] in the Old; the Old is made accessible [*patet*] by the New." We may compare this classical play on words with a contemporary example. Richard Hays has this to say: "In the first lecture, I proposed the twofold thesis that the OT teaches us how to read the Gospels and that—at the same time—the Gospels teach us how to read the OT. The hermeneutical key to this intertextual dialectic is the practice of *figural reading*."[8] Teachers of the early church termed this kind of Biblical reading "typology" after Rom 5:14, showing how those latent features (*latet*) of the OT become patent (*patet*) in Jesus. For Jesus pulls the whole Story together—so Luke 24:25–27; indeed, he is shown to be not only the *climax* of the Story but even the *premise* of the Story! E.g. John 1:1, 8:58, 1 Cor 8:4–6, Col 1:15–20, Heb 1:1–4. Re this last reference from Hebrews: "the new *corresponds* to the old, but *surpasses* it, and does so absolutely, by providing the *perfection* of the true, spiritual order" (Harold Attridge commenting on Hebrews).[9] And so we may come full circle, with a comment from Henri de Lubac, which itself concludes by referencing Origen's αὐτοβασιλεία in a note, as above:

---

as he is wisdom itself and righteousness itself and truth itself, so too is he also the kingdom itself [*autobasileia*]. But it is not a kingdom over the things below or over a part of the things above, but over all things above which have been called heaven. And if you are searching for the meaning of "theirs is the kingdom of heaven" (Mt 5:3), you can say theirs is Christ since he is the *kingdom itself*..."

8. Hays, *Reading Backwards*, 93, emphasis original. Both the opening chapter of *Reading Backwards* and the Introduction of *Gospel Echoes* elaborate further what it means to interpret Israel's Scriptures via such figural reading. For those who wish to follow matters even further, see Ribbens, "Typology of Types: Typology in Dialogue," where he rehearses the relationship between figural reading and the more traditional form of typology.

9. Attridge, cited in Webster, "One Who Is Son," 74, emphases original.

The intimate links between the two Testaments are of quite another kind. Within the very consciousness of Jesus—if we may cast a human glance into that sanctuary—the Old Testament was seen as the matrix of the New or as the instrument of its creation. This meant something much more than extrinsic preparation. Even the categories used by Jesus to tell us about himself are ancient biblical categories. Jesus causes them to burst forth or, if you prefer, *sublimates them and unifies them by making them converge upon himself.*[10]

---

10. De Lubac, "Spiritual Understanding," 7, emphasis added.

Part Three (Session 4)

Full Immersion in the Rule of God's Life

Luke-Acts

Getting involved, becoming incorporated into the history of God's supreme action in his world, sharing in the divine economy—this is what, in brief, the NT offers us and what this session will begin to introduce. And there are essentially three strands to this involvement, this incorporation—this *baptism*. The story of **Acts 2:1–39** is the key, the climax of which is vv. 38–39 (NIV):

> Peter replied, "Repent and be baptized, every one of you, in the name of Jesus Christ for the forgiveness of your sins. And you will receive the gift of the Holy Spirit. The promise is for you and for your children and for all who are far off—for all whom the Lord our God might call."

Historically, various parts of the church have accentuated different aspects of Peter's call:

▶ Repent	Evangelicals
▶ Be baptized	Sacramentalists
▶ The gift of the Holy Spirit	Pentecostals

These three indispensable avenues to participating in the history/story of God's action in Jesus originally formed *a single and strong cord of Christian initiation*. Over time, however, down through the

PART THREE (SESSION 4): FULL IMMERSION IN THE RULE OF GOD'S LIFE

centuries, they became unraveled, so that we are often presented nowadays with what appear to be *three competing streams* of Christian tradition. Yet the story of Christian origins would disagree! In other words, if we are to more fully appreciate and enjoy the entire wealth of what God has done through Jesus and in the Holy Spirit, then we need to bring these three strands or threads back together.

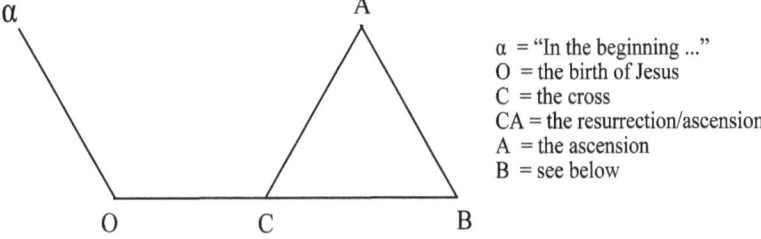

Figure 4: A representation of the Economy derived from Luke–Acts

Luke's two volume work, what we know as his Gospel and Acts, helps us here. We need to notice that Luke tells the story of the ascension *twice*, once at the *conclusion* of his Gospel and again as the *introduction* to Acts. This is because the ascension is a *hinge event*: it marks the end of Jesus' own earthly career—he is a human glorified, in the presence of the eternal Father; and it initiates the disciples (and the whole church) into sharing what he has done. For Luke deliberately writes *two volumes*, so rich and expansive is God's economy of salvation.

In the Book of Acts, the One who was in the Gospel story, "the Man of the Spirit" (notably **Luke 1:35, 3:21–22, 4:1, 14–21**), becomes now "the Lord of the Spirit,"[1] "the One who baptizes in Holy Spirit" (John 1:33). Yet it is exactly at this point that we should be most careful regarding just this "baptismal" language. In **Luke 24:49** the Spirit is called "the Father's promise" and is associated with "power." Read **Acts 1:1–11**. Acts 1:4 repeats the language of promise, and verse 5 takes up John's prediction of Luke 3:16, but reverses an active verb into a passive, leaving the subject, the baptizing one, unspecified for now. Incidentally, Acts 1:8 deliberately

---

1. Dunn, *Baptism*, 41.

echoes **Luke 1:35,** where both use the rare, unusual compound verb ἐπέρχομαι (*epi* + *erchomai*: upon + to come), while also ringing the changes with the words "Holy Spirit" and "power." This *explicitly ties together the beginnings of these two volumes*: aO is deliberately *parallel* to AB above.

Finally, at crucial stages in the Book of Acts the activity of the Spirit is depicted by Luke's ringing the changes once more, using eight different phrases overall: baptize in the Holy Spirit (HSp); the HSp comes upon; being filled with the HSp; pour out the HSp; receive (the gift of) the HSp; give (the gift of) the HSp; the HSp falls upon; the promise of the HSp. That is, we need not and should not get too hung up on the actual *expression* "baptism in/with the Holy Spirit." What is crucial is the actual *reality* to which the expression refers, notably in terms of the summary description offered in Acts 2:38–39. And what is that reality, do you think?

ABC = the "overwhelming/drenching" work of the Holy Spirit whereby we are "put into" Jesus' entire work, OCA (**Acts 2:33; Rom 6:3; 1 Cor 12:13; Col 2:9–12**). The English word "baptism" comes directly from the Greek word *baptizein*, which means immerse, drench, overwhelm, plunge, dip, put into. In other words, what Jesus did formally in his own life in a substitutionary and representative manner is now actualized for each person/household who comes to him. A kind of "recycling" occurs, as Jesus "immerses" people into himself with/by means of the Holy Spirit, *the self-same One* who enabled his own mission.

It is important to see all this activity represented by these lines as the ministry of the glorified Jesus Christ, in the presence of the eternal Father, through the eternal Holy Spirit (see Heb 9:14). Otherwise, to indicate diagrammatically a supposed "movement backwards in time," the line BC (for the disciples some thirty-five years and less, for ourselves around two thousand), and to see all the events of Jesus' career in the power of the Spirit from conception to exaltation, OCA, as "telescoped into a single happening" is perhaps rather confusing.

Yet something like this way of speaking, coupled with the diagrammatic lines, is meaningful when we see the transcendent

Part Three (Session 4): Full Immersion in the Rule of God's Life

Lord of History breaking into history and himself becoming an actor in the drama (*the* Singular Actor!) and proleptically and programmatically establishing his sovereign rule. On the one hand, there are three elements or phases to the climax of the economy of salvation: the events of Jesus' mission; the ensuing era of the Church; the Parousia (which repeats key features of N. T. Wright's scheme of the "Five Acts," which constitute the Divine Story contained in the entire Bible—Creation, Fall, Israel, Jesus, and Church).[2] On the other hand, this division is to a large degree more analytical than real. For the experience of the church since Pentecost is a "recycling" of what has *already* happened to our substitute and representative human being, Jesus; and the Parousia, or Second Coming, is the Unveiling and Appearing of what *already* is the case "in Christ Jesus" (see, for example, Col 3:3–4 and 1 Pet 1:3–9). While the Old Age is still with us, although passing away and destined to perish, the New Age of God's future, the New Creation, has arrived/begun to arrive and *we can share in it already*, in union with Christ Jesus. Recall the diagrams of last time, especially the Christian fulfillment, noting now the Old Age has an arrow for time's continuance, while the New doesn't (something else temporal is afoot!):

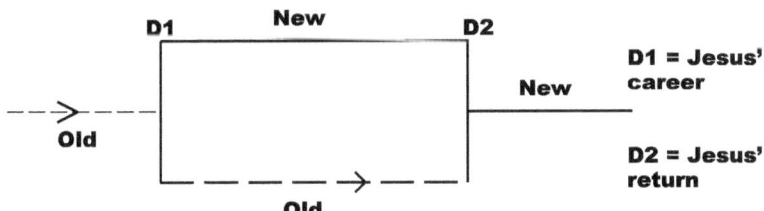

Figure 5: The Christian Fulfilment (once more)

In this context, when we display the fullness of what God has done in Jesus and by means of the Holy Spirit, our own participation, our own immersion in the story/drama, needs to acknowledge

---

2. Wright's Five Act scheme is introduced in *New Testament*, 141–43, to which we should add a sixth act, Consummation, or the Parousia/Second Coming.

all three elements highlighted by Peter in Acts 2. To be sure, one of the points of Luke's selection of the major experiences of the Spirit's action in the story of the Book of Acts is to show yet again that God himself rings the changes on *the sequence of events*. In some cases, repentance comes first and the Spirit last; in others the Spirit is dramatically to the fore and water baptism last. It seems the *order* in which these three necessary elements occur in any given situation does not exactly matter. Rather, what does matter is that *we embrace all three* respectively in their fullness, so that we know overall the very fullness of what God has done in Jesus and the Holy Spirit.

Questions for Reflection

10. Of the three dimensions of Christian Initiation, with which one(s) do you feel most familiar and from which one(s) might you be most alienated?

11. How might you/we cultivate a richer sense of the latter? And how might you integrate them more fully with the former?

12. Yes, the temporal consequences of the Gospel are most puzzling, stretching the mind beyond its normal capacities. For while the Old Age of sin and death surely continues in our midst, so too is the reality of Jesus' resurrection, and so is his new creation, properly present, here and now. "Somehow" the future of God's purposes has arrived/begun to arrive from out of that future and has invaded our present—even as the old aeon persists, and tenaciously so. This teasing juxtaposition presents the puzzling dynamic of what it means for the triune God to redeem from *within* history, through Jesus, God Incarnate, and the Holy Spirit, who is himself the ἀρραβών (*arrabōn*), the deposit or "guarantee of [that very future] inheritance until we acquire possession of it." (Eph 1:14 RSV).

PART THREE (SESSION 5)

Abiding in the Rule of God's Life

Baptism and Eucharist

If we begin well, we may also continue well—and especially like this. Let's recall our first diagram depicting God's action via Jesus and the Spirit, now with a small addition:

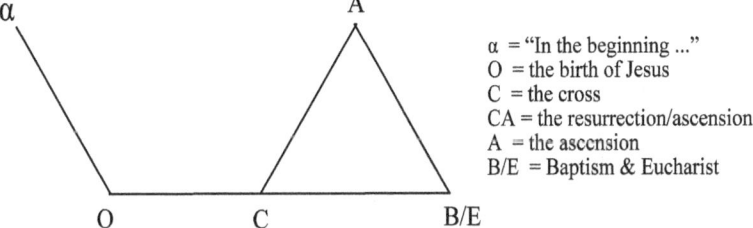

α = "In the beginning ..."
O = the birth of Jesus
C = the cross
CA = the resurrection/ascension
A = the ascension
B/E = Baptism & Eucharist

Figure 6: Luke-Acts revised displaying both dominical sacraments

Down the centuries there has been considerable controversy surrounding the business of *water baptism*. Much heat and not too much light has emanated from the pages and pages of spilled ink on the sundry "positions"! Entire churches have split apart over what in fact amounts to partial and inadequate vision of how the Christian Life begins—and how it might better continue. Pentecostals have split from Baptists, and Evangelicals have castigated Sacramentalists. Just so, the very factionalism

31

that Paul seeks to address in **1 Cor 1:10-16** rears its head again. To be sure, there *are* genuine differences here, so that **1 Cor 11:18-19** also has impact still. The remaining question is only how to stand sufficiently far away to gain an adequate perspective (historical and theological) on all these controversial matters. God be praised! The church experiences and newfound/revived understandings of the last century have offered us a wholesome, genuine way forward—at last!

The trap extreme Evangelicals (for want of a better label) fall into is to *abstract* the *point* B from the *line* ABC in figure 6 above, while equally the trap excessive Sacramentalists fall into is to *collapse* the *line* onto the *point* itself. The truth is that B *is* indeed *part* of this very line—we may not *separate off* water baptism from the overall process of becoming Christian—while B is also *only* a part and *not* the *entire* line—water baptism is not *all* there is to becoming a Christian. And finally, the Pentecostal revival of the twentieth century and the charismatic renewal thereafter correctly allude to the *fullness* of what God has done and does in Jesus through the Spirit, even as they customarily *misappropriate* only *one* form of NT language to indicate this *awesomely rich reality*. The upshot: there is our own individual part to play (Evangelicals); there is the Christian community's part to play (Sacramentalists); and there is God's part to play (Pentecostals). As and when *each* strand is *woven together with* the *others*, so we have a sufficiently strong cord of Christian beginnings—*from which* we may grow and mature.

Summary

A certain Tom Torrance offers a good conclusion to these considerations, commenting on Cyril of Alexandria (412–444):

> Worship belongs to the whole sphere of life in Christ, in which we are justified in the Spirit through union with Christ, and not by the works of the law or of the flesh....

Part Three (Session 5): Abiding in the Rule of God's Life

Cyril goes out of his way to stress the *noetic* or *spiritual* nature of Christian worship in sacrifice and sacrament, contrasted with the external and physical rites of the Old Covenant. That does not import the rejection of physical acts in liturgical worship, or of the need to embody devotion in deeds and good works, but rather the rejection of *institutional substitutes* for worship of God in spirit and in truth. **After the glorification of Christ and the coming of the Spirit liturgical acts have essentially *a typical and indicative function*, for they direct us to the actual *leitourgia* and *latreia*, which Christ fulfilled on our behalf.**[1]

In other words, both word and sacrament function as do "the Scriptures" in **John 5:39–40** by referring directly to Jesus *himself* (he is *the* Living Word, while they are written words). Similarly, the "signs" (selected miraculous deeds in the Fourth Gospel), which, though real in themselves (bread is eaten by the hungry, a blind man is given sight), are premonitions of Jesus' own Glory enacted through the Hour (I am the Bread of Life, the true Bread from heaven, I am the Light of the World); they testify to/signify this Glory being manifested and effected through the cross and resurrection. Chapters 1–12, which may be designated the Book of Signs, precede chapters 13–20, the Book of Glory, just as most of the long discourses (which consist of *words* n.b.) follow the signs, since they need true explanation. That is, the full meaning of the climactic Hour of Jesus' mission from the Father, in cross and resurrection, may only be truly accessed via "word-&-sacrament"/"Scripture-&-sign," for he himself is Lamb of God and Great High Priest (John 1:29, chapter 17; Heb 3:1, 2:3b–4) on our behalf—*if only we might perceive it to be so*, with the eyes of faith, and the inspiration and realization of the Spirit from above (John 3:1–15, 6:63).

One final and wonderful thing: what the rite of baptism *initiates*, by signifying and embodying—our immersion into the very Life of God with/through Jesus in the Spirit—the Eucharistic rite

---

1. Torrance, "Mind of Christ," 179–80 (last sentence emphasis added, while other emphases original). *Leitourgia* = bringing of offerings or performing ceremonial services; *latreia* = worship/service of God.

continues/maintains ("nourishes" is Calvin's word). It's as simple and direct as that! See the interchangeability of B/E above. For we must note well *both* the characteristic Johannine verb, μένειν (*menein* = abide/continue/dwell/remain/stay), in **John 6:56**, *and* Paul's key word, κοινωνία (*koinōnia* = fellowship/communion/communication, *the* hallmark of the Holy Spirit, hence the line AEC), in 1 **Cor 10:16–17**.[2] Sadly, we Western Christians in the Latin tradition, who have not kept the practice and theology of the *epiclesis* alive as have the Eastern churches, are at a disadvantage here [*epi* = upon; *kaleō* = I call, literally, we "call upon the Holy Spirit" in the liturgy to fall upon (AEC again) the congregation/assembly/church to have "communion" with/renewed participation in Jesus' life, death, resurrection and ascension (OCA) by means of the Holy Spirit-and-the-action-with-the-elements-of-bread-and-wine; for by these means, the glorified Son of Man grants believers to eat the true living bread from heaven, his flesh for the life of the world].[3] Yet God be praised here too! For the last century saw a great revival of liturgical understanding of Eastern and Western, Greek and Latin traditions, as developed originally by the undivided early church's worship. Here is a rich tradition which delightfully integrates with what Pentecostals also know full well, God's Powerful and Empowering Presence among his people as they gather together,[4] but now with added riches on account of the liturgical cross-fertilization.

> Christ, our Passover lamb, has been sacrificed. So let us keep the Feast, not with the old yeast, the yeast of malice and wickedness, but with the unleavened bread of sincerity and truth (1 Cor 5:7–8 NRSV/NIV). Let us come and believe in Wisdom Incarnate, who sets before us the True Passover Feast through his Words of eternal life that we may eat the flesh and drink the blood of the glorified Son of Man to abide/dwell in him and he in us (John

---

2. See Pitre, *Jesus and the Last Supper*, for a comprehensive discussion of the first century Jewish setting of this basic rite, with its motifs of New Passover, New Exodus, and New Covenant as the primary matrix for our understanding—despite perhaps inadequate frameworks thereafter.

3. See McKenna, *Eucharist and Holy Spirit*.

4. See Fee, *God's Empowering Presence*.

6:35–69), as we remember/proclaim his death until he comes (1 Cor 11:26).

Questions for Reflection

13. Ministry of word-and-sacrament (Scripture-and-sign): which of this pair might you gravitate most naturally toward, and which demur from, and why? Are you an attentive ministry-of-the-word sort of person? Or do you prefer the more ritual-sacramental kind of services? How might we integrate them more fully? And finally, how do you understand and experience the Holy Spirit to manifest Jesus Christ through these means—and through other means as well?

14. Bill Burnett, an ex-Archbishop of Cape Town, once remarked, "The problem with the Anglican Church is that we have superimposed a sacramental structure upon an unevangelized people." One suspects this problem to be applicable to many traditions who overemphasize the sacramental to the detriment of the evangelical. What do you think of this assessment?

15. The Eucharistic rite has provoked a divergence of understandings over the centuries, from, for example, Thomas Aquinas through to Zwingli (in the West). How might this session (and its references) reformulate our basic approach to the matter?

16. There is a certain irony in the fact that the two key sacraments of baptism and Eucharist are meant to declare an essential unity among the people of God, and yet their current practice and understanding would seemingly contradict this. What do you think a more fulsome understanding and experience of the triune God's economy of salvation might do to remedy this? See especially *LDL* chapter 8. Appendix 3 also details 'A way of "reading" the sacrament of the Eucharist,' which helps to address Questions 15 and 16.

17. By way of a summary conclusion, sessions 1–5 have presented the economy of salvation from Abraham to its climax in Jesus. Its complex story line has revealed a rich tapestry of threads and how they might all come together to display Jesus, the Messiah of Israel and God Incarnate. But it does not end there. God's economy precisely seeks to embrace human beings—indeed, the entire world—with the church as the first fruits of the triune God's new creation.

    Yet as we've been led down this Way of Salvation, as narrated through Scripture's testimony, the suspicion is that perhaps one's/our glimpse of this drama is somewhat partial. Perhaps not all the motifs of the narrative have been given their due weight; perhaps some have even dropped out of sight. Just so, the next session casts a vision of the fullness of the intent of the triune God. And thereafter from this perspective, how we might better and more fully live with this triune God.

Part Four (Session 6)

Growing into the Fullness of God's Life

Having laid the foundations well, we are now ready to build high. Once more, the NT offers us rich means for this building process. We begin with **Eph 1–3** to set the scene, to whet the appetite.

Chapter 1

Vv. 3–14   *A threefold paean of praise to the glory of the triune God*

- for God the Father's eternal will and loving purposes (vv. 3–6)
- for executing this plan through Jesus, who "heads it all up" (vv. 7–12)

    (n.b., the word *oikonomia* (1:10) expresses "God's Story/Drama" in a nutshell—see below)

- for the Holy Spirit, who seals us, guaranteeing the final fulfillment of all God's purposes (vv. 13–14)[1]

---

1. We should note the Spirit is described as the ἀρραβών (*arrabōn*), the deposit or "guarantee of our inheritance until we acquire possession of it" (RSV), which he *may be* towards us, his creatures, since he *is* among the triune Godhead God's very own Unsurpassable Futurity. See *LDL*, page 69 and note 40, and more expansively chapter 7 on "Temporality," 117–37.

37

Vv. 15–23   *Prayer for the full realization* of *what has been effected* by *the trinitarian God*

"insight" → "knowledge" → "vision" → "knowledge", so that we might *see and understand*:

- the hope (future) of our calling (past): comprehensiveness! (vv. 13–14 regarding the Spirit; vv. 3–6 regarding the Father)
- inheritance again (v. 14)
- immeasurable greatness of power, energizing, strong, might—all exhibited by . . .
- *the criterion* of it all: fullness (Augustine of Hippo referred to 1:22–23 as "the Whole Christ"; see *LDL*, page 78, as well as note 60)

Chapter 2

Vv. 1–10   "But God . . . "—*The Great Reversal in Christ Jesus*

the significance of *our* incorporation *into Christ Jesus*, the One of whom so much has been said and extolled so far. (Once again, what are the roles of water baptism, faith, and the Holy Spirit?)

Vv. 11–22   Further *implications* of our reunion with the Father through the Son and in the Holy Spirit (2:18)

a dwelling place for all

For the triune God, men, women, strangers, friends, Jew, Gentile, slave, free, rich, poor, black, white, east, west, north, south, etc.[2]

2. See again Perrin, *Jesus the Temple*, notably chapter 2, "'Don't you know that you yourselves are the temple of God?' The early Church as a counter-temple movement," 46–79. Note that this view of Perrin's is properly basic: once Jesus identifies himself as the new, eschatological temple, thereafter his followers, those who constitute his Body, being "baptized into him," are similarly and properly *the* locus of God's Presence in the world. See also 1

PART FOUR (SESSION 6): GROWING INTO THE FULLNESS OF GOD'S LIFE

Some necessary Greek details to get the point regarding οἶκος/ *oikos*, which means house/household/dwelling. The scheme of Paul's thought in this section assumes the overall imagery of the OT temple building and its sacrificial system; see session 2 above, with the entire OT cult being fulfilled in Jesus, as portrayed by e.g. John's Gospel, session 3. Ephesians 2 then elaborates this theme of Jesus and the Temple, the "fullness" of the Divine Presence. For perhaps not surprisingly, our EVV miss this deliberate catena of cognate Greek words:

1:10, 3:2,9	οἰκονομία/*oikonomia*	= management of a household, stewardship, a plan
	οἰκονόμος/*oikonomos*	= steward, manager
2:19	οἰκεῖος/*oikeios*	= pertaining to a household or family
	οἰκοδομέω/*oikodomeō*	= build (repair, amplify, advance)
2:20	ἐπι + οἰκοδομέω/*epi*	= build *upon*
2:21, 4:16	οἰκοδομή/*oikodomē*	= a building
2:22	συν + οἰκοδομέω/*sun + oikodomeō*	= build *together with*
2:22	κατοικητήριον/*katoikētērion*	= habitation, dwelling place

Chapter 3

Vv. 1, 14–21   *"For this reason . . ."*

Links directly back to the previous verses regarding the Gentile inclusion in God's commonwealth, the fulfillment of his purposes (recall Gen 12:3). Yet, the prayer itself, arising from what has gone before, in order that folk would "actually get it," does not appear until v. 14, and so . . .

Cor 3:9–11, 16–17, 6:19–20; 2 Cor 6:16; 1 Pet 2:4–10; and the Letter to the Hebrews generally, climaxing in Rev 21–22.

39

Vv. 2–13 are therefore a *digression* on Paul's understanding of his own calling and how he fulfilled it, and notably regarding the very inclusion of these Gentiles

Vv. 2–7 are one sentence; vv. 8–12 a second, with v. 13 the conclusion, harking back to Paul's being a "prisoner of Christ Jesus" (v. 1), being the specific form of apostolic "suffering" (v. 13) involved in executing his ministry for "you Gentiles."

- "grace given to me" (vv. 2, 7, 8)
- "the mystery" of the Gospel of Christ with which Paul is entrusted (vv. 3, 4, 9) . . .
- . . . which is "made known/revealed" through Paul (vv. 3, 5, 10).
- Note the sheer autobiographical style: "I", "me," and "my"; all regarding "You Gentiles."

Question for Reflection

18. To what specific ministry has God "commissioned" you? What are you called to steward within the economy of the triune God of grace?

- who are "co-heirs" [Greek: *sun*], in "same body" [*sun*], "co-sharers" [*sun*] (v. 6)
- thus are the Apostle Paul, the gospel, and the church *all thoroughly intertwined*
- so that, vv. 11 and 12 breathe the same formal, rhythmic liturgical language of 1:3–14

> All of this reinforces the *unity/oneness* and *catholicity/wholeness* of the church.

PART FOUR (SESSION 6): GROWING INTO THE FULLNESS OF GOD'S LIFE

Compare all this with **Col 1:24-28** regarding suffering, apostleship, revelation of a hidden mystery, content of the mystery, proclamation of this content.

The digression therefore underscores the need for . . .

Vv. 14-21   *a second prayer for the realization* of what is the case "in Christ Jesus" and "the church": this time, that *everything* which has come from the Father might be *cashed out, put into effect*

- the petition is utterly trinitarian: before the Father, in the Spirit, that Christ . . .
- Father/familyhood = *the* singular *Source* of *all* = comprehensive unity as well
- *three* specific requests are made, each beginning with "that" vv. 16, 18, 19b
- requests 1 and 2 each have similar patterns:
- a single main idea—grant/empower →
- two infinitives—strengthen and dwell (parallel ideas) → being rooted and grounded
- two infinitives—comprehend/grasp and know (again parallel) → . . .

Such is the immensity and incomprehensibility of God's wisdom and love in Christ as shown on the Cross that this knowledge and power and love are surely way beyond any human capacities, undergirding previous references to the need for the mystery to be revealed/made known: just so, the prayer itself!

- request number 3 = the most awesome outcome!
  We've come full circle regarding the criterion of fullness.
- concluding doxology, including over-the-top superlatives in the original Greek, binding all together.

Questions for Reflection

19. The English words "realization/to realize" have a specific two-fold meaning: to see and understand/come to know, and to cash out/bring into effect. It is no coincidence the two prayers in this Letter to the Ephesians, 1:15-23 and 3:14-21, respectively encapsulate these two meanings perfectly.

20. In what ways might we, together as the community of the church, better pray these two prayers; and then expect the triune God to answer them?

21. A key, and perhaps *the* key, form of an answer will be in the triune God's Coming to *dwell* among his people. From the cosmic temple of Gen 1 through the erecting of tabernacle and temple (and their subsequent destruction) in the OT and on to Ezekiel's visionary temple, culminating in Jesus' own "tabernacling" among us, with his own subsequent crucifixion and resurrection—all this seeks fulfillment in Eph 2:11-22, the true *totus Christus, the* Divine Presence. All of which also leads us into the next series of reflections.

22. Prayer and worship is always the first avenue into living with the Trinity. Consequently, please reread *LDL* chapter 5. If you haven't a copy of the book to hand, then read **Luke 11:1-13**, and then **1 Cor 8:4-6**. Both of these illustrate the necessary trinitarian grammar of prayer and worship, the latter based on the Jewish *Shema*, which Paul seems to modify so naturally in the light of Jesus' Coming.

23. "The doctrine of the Trinity *is* doxological acknowledgment: 'Glory to God, Father, Son, and Holy Spirit; as in the beginning, so now, and forever. Amen!' is the confessional cry of the whole of creation!" (*LDL*, pages 165-6, the conclusion to chapter 9). How has this study of Ephesians in this session and its presentation of the economy of salvation endorsed this conclusion for you?

Part Four (Session 6): Growing into the Fullness of God's Life

24. The next sessions will then fill out the consequences of this doxology by means of Eph 4:17—6:20 and the NT Catechetical form. For here we are offered a quite specific form of life, which unfolds for us the nature of living with the triune God and God's dwelling among humanity.

Part Four (Session 7)

Growing into the Fullness of God's Life

The New Testament Catechism

Most are agreed that Christian initiation is the primary avenue into and setting for the Trinity. Baptism in the threefold name, Father, Son, and Holy Spirit (Matt 28:19), is the first human encounter of life begun with the triune God. Yet parts 1–3 have suggested this simple summary invokes, in fact, a profoundly rich contextual background: the drama of God's salvation is uniquely immeasurable. Our first session of part 4, using Ephesians, acted as something of a hinge. It paved the Way with something of a backcloth summary of the economy (chapters 1–3), before the rest of the letter embarks upon an extensive elaboration of the significance of entering down this Way as it uses the most complete NT example of the baptismal catechetical form (chapters 4–6).

At least four verses in the epistles suggest that very early the church had a set pattern of basic teaching, by means of which it instructed its members. **Rom 6:17** says that the Roman Christians "had obeyed from the heart (the) form of teaching to which (they) were committed/handed over." E.G. Selwyn remarks, "The phrase connotes a limited course of instruction, which followed definite and settled lines."[1] Commentators suggest that both **Eph 4:20–21**

---

1. Selwyn, *First Epistle*, 389. The rest of part 4 follows particularly his Essay II, 365–466.

Part Four (Session 7): Growing into the Fullness of God's Life

and **Col 2:6–7** also allude to a given form of catechism, in which people "learned Christ." More obvious is **2 Tim 1:13**, which Selwyn paraphrases: "Have (i.e., have by you) a sketch or outline of the sound words you have heard from me, in the study we have had together of Christian faith and conduct (love)."[2] Overall, the NT *baptisma*, with its three elements—evangelical, sacramental and Pentecostal—precipitates a quite specific "form of teaching," which is evidenced throughout many parts of the Epistles. They are scattered throughout like tips of an iceberg, yet this only begs an enquiry into digging below the waterline to access and reconstruct the whole.

Selwyn's reconstruction runs as follows:

(i) Entry into the new (Christian) life:

    a. its basis—the word of truth, the gospel

    b. its nature—rebirth, new creation, new humanity, light (from darkness)

(ii) The new life: renunciation and abstentions; its negative implications

(iii) The new life: its faith and worship

(iv) The new life: its positive virtues and duties—holiness, love and submission, to God and each other

(v) Because of "worldly" reaction: watch and pray—persecution, suffering, and trials are the expected birth pangs of the messianic Kingdom; and so . . .

(vi) Stand—against the Evil One. God will arm and establish the Christian in the face of "crisis"

---

2. Ibid., 401. It is on account of Webster's use of Ursinus's use of 2 Tim 1:13 that this workbook is constructed the way it is: see Webster, *Holy Scripture*, 112–16, "Scripture and catechesis".

The Sections of the Catechism

I As we've seen, entry into the New Life is by means of Jesus baptizing people with/in the Holy Spirit into himself (notably session 4). He personally is the fulfillment of God's entire economy as narrated during the course of the Holy Scriptures (sessions 1–3 especially, and **2 Cor 1:19b-20**). His word of promise now seeks our human response in "the obedience of faith" (Rom 1:5, 16:26), our human "yes" to the gracious initiative and invitation of God (**Luke 1:37-38, 8:19-21; Acts 1:14**).

See too Acts 2:38-39, 20:21; Mark 1:14-15; John 20:31; 1 John 1:1-5; 2 Cor 6:1-2; Col 1:13-14; Jas 1:18; 1 Pet 1:23, 1:3-5.

II–IV Eph 4:20-24 (NRSV) illustrate these sections delightfully.

That is not the way you learned Christ! For surely you have heard about him and were taught in him, as the truth is in Jesus. You were taught to put away your former way of life, your old self [literally, man], corrupt and deluded by its lusts, and to be renewed in the spirit of your minds, and to clothe yourselves with the new self, created according to the likeness of God in true righteousness and holiness.

This archetypal pairing of *putting off* the *old* and *putting on* the *new* (see **Col 3:1-14**), "in the power of the Spirit" (Rom 8:13), via the "renewing of the spirit of the mind," may be likened to a pair of scissors. Such an instrument is made up of three things: a pair of opposing blades, and a rivet holding them together. This crucial pivot, with a similar contrast of old and new, is exactly what Paul presents again at the turning point of his magisterial **Romans, 12:1-2** (NRSV/NIV):

Part Four (Session 7): Growing into the Fullness of God's Life

> I appeal to you therefore, brothers and sisters, in view of God's mercies, to present your bodies as a living sacrifice, holy and acceptable to God, which is your spiritual/ reasonable worship. Do not be conformed to this world [*aeon*], but be transformed by the renewing of your mind, so that you may test and approve what God's will is—his good, pleasing and perfect will.

Here "worship" is far more than those occasions when Christians gather together, however important these may be. For the point is this: for good or ill, we become like what we worship. The image of a pair of scissors allows us to probe the deep connections between a due noetic Christian sense of worship with its faithful, lived acknowledgement of the Reality of the One true triune God (the pivot), and the necessary moral, ethical, and virtuous embodiments of that worship in due Christian character (the blades), as the church and its members live *in* the world/this age and *for* the world but not *of* the world/this age. Just so, specifically, we cannot face the world in Christian mission unless we have first faced God in worship; yet the authenticity of that worship is tested by the reality of our mission. And generically, our entering into God's mission for the world is our entering into the worship of God, which mission is justly celebrated in the church's liturgy. And so finally, as the Great Thanksgiving prayer concludes, "Through him and with him and in him [Jesus], in the power of the Holy Spirit, all honor and glory be to you, Almighty Father, now and forever!"

What kinds of Christian gathering (in a liturgical setting, but not only there) may best "view" just these "divine mercies," molding our vision and our life to the One true God of authentic human worship? In the language of Eph 1:15–18a, what forms of prayer and praise may best offer our full realization of what has been effected by the trinitarian God (Eph 1:3–14), in true "insight," leading to "knowledge," leading to "vision," leading to "knowledge"—namely, of the *Risen Presence* of the Lord Jesus Christ in all his mighty power and authority *among* his people, as head of his body?

By way of answer, we should note firstly the close parallels between "letting the Spirit fill [us]" (**Eph 5:18**) and "letting the

Word of Christ/the Lord/God dwell in [us] richly" (**Col 3:16**). For the consequences of each are, respectively, 5:19–21 (NRSV modified) and 3:16–17 (NRSV modified):

> [S]inging psalms and hymns and spiritual songs among yourselves, singing and making melody to the Lord in your hearts, giving thanks to God the Father at all times and for everything in the name of our Lord Jesus Christ, submitting yourselves to one another out of reverence for Christ.

> [T]eaching and admonishing one another in all wisdom; and with gratitude in your hearts, singing psalms, hymns, and spiritual songs to God. And whatever you do, in word or deed, doing everything in the name of the Lord Jesus, giving thanks to God the Father through him.

So, the forms of the Church's life, *in providing for worship*, must foster just these *opportunities for the Word's and the Holy Spirit's ministries*, to conform folks (back) into the image of Christ in the power of the Spirit, as their goal. Any ministry is in the first instance that of word-and-sacrament, Scripture-and-sign, among God's gathered people, to equip them (ordinary Christians) and knit them together, for growth in *their* ministry and mission in the Father's world which Jesus came to redeem (Eph 4:11–16).

Question for Reflection

25. What then of your own times together? How do they foster such growth in holiness and love through the Word and the Spirit?

Submission

At the core of the Christian revelation is the triune personal God whose very relations *are* the self-communication of the divine toward humanity, which finds supreme expression in the hymn we have as **Phil 2:6–11** (**read 1–13** overall: the NRSV translation is by far the best at catching the Greek sense here). We said earlier

Part Four (Session 7): Growing into the Fullness of God's Life

that the scandal of Jesus' Coming was due to the Baptizer having to become the Baptized One, or the Judge (of the Day of Yahweh) the Judged One. Now we may equally say, the Lord of all has become the humble and humiliated Servant of all. This is the revelation of Jesus. For only the Servant of all may be the sovereign Lord of all, such is the true identity of the God of "grace and truth" (John 1:14). This is the absolute crux of the Christian revelation, of the Gospel of Jesus.

See **Isa 52:13, 6:1, 57:15, 45:22–23, 48:11**, and **53:12**, linked with *the baptismal voice* (**Matt 3:17**, see earlier sessions for the three OT texts). See also **John 3:14–15, 8:28**, and **12:32–34**. Note the expression "lifted up" has a typical double meaning in John— *both* hoisted up off the ground on a Roman gibbet, *and* raised from the grave by God—so that the meaning of "glory" (**see John 12:23** and **13:31–32** [Isa 40:3–5 ties in with John 12:32], and chapter 17's prayer) is likewise double-edged. (By the way, Isa 44:6 and 48:12 tie in with Rev 1:8, 17, 2:8, 21:6, and 22:13 as well, such is the richness of the book of Isaiah as a Christian resource.)

As a result, it is not surprising that any due immersion into *such a God's life* will have that *form of life* reflected among those who share it among themselves. Just so, the final feature of "being filled with the Holy Spirit" is "*submitting yourselves to one another out of reverence for Christ*" (**Eph 5:18–21**).[3] What this concretely means is then tabled by *three pairs of relationships* that exemplify the extended households of the first century (see section iv in the table above). In our day, of course, there is much uproar concerning "emancipation," generated by a desire for a form of "freedom" that would seek just such an *escape* from any "mutual submission." For "freedom" is *my* "right" to "choose" whatsoever is good in my own eyes; it is my own self-authenticating, self-positing act which ensures my very identity, my preference that is my lifestyle, my very own self determination. And while the world of the postmodern undergirds such a nihilistic drive to fragmentation, the Gospel of

---

3. We should note that most English Bibles begin a new paragraph at v. 21, though this is neither necessary nor preferable. For v. 18's imperative, "be filled" is followed by a string of participles climaxing with "submitting," displaying the various *results or consequences* of being filled with the Spirit.

Jesus Christ would offer something rather different. Stated briefly, freedom is a collective and so relational matter: your freedom is my gift to you, my freedom is your gift to me, etc., all granted/authorised by Another (see *LDL*, pages 185–6, and question 28, page 191). For at the Gospel's heart is the nuptial mystery (Eph 5:32), the relationship of "One flesh" that is the spousal bonding of Christ and his church, the *totus Christus* as Augustine would once again call the whole reality (Eph 1:22–23), where the heartbeat of such a mutual relationship is "mutual submission."

Yet, such a *self emptying before another* is *precisely the form of relationship* enjoyed by the trinitarian God; such *are* the very relationships of Father, Son, and Holy Spirit that *is* the Life of the Trinity, as each "glorifies" the Other(s)—so the Fourth Gospel's language. This is the form of life manifested by the Living God of Glory, whose Lordship *is* service, whose Name *is* Jesus.

> For thus says the High and Exalted One who lives eternally and whose name is holy, "I live in the holy heights, but I am with the contrite and humble, to revive the spirit of the humble, to revive the heart of the contrite." (Isa 57:15 NIV)

Just so has the Father raised this *Crucified* Jesus from the dead in the glory of the Spirit and has given him the Name (Yahweh = God's Name) above all heights and through all ages, the same yesterday, today, and forever! And just so, we have confidence to approach boldly this throne of grace.

See Phil 2:9–11; Heb 4:16, 10:19–25; and *LDL*, 20–24, for more on Philippians.[4]

---

4. Watch/listen together to: https://www.youtube.com/watch?v=nQWFzMvCfLE

PART FOUR (SESSION 7): GROWING INTO THE FULLNESS OF GOD'S LIFE

Questions for Reflection

26. The old is rendered old precisely by "the emergence of the new":[5] and so for you, how has this "new" cast its sway over your life? What has been rendered "old"? What sort of thinking patterns and kinds of activities have you had to change in light of Jesus' cross and resurrection and your own incorporation into him? What has been put to death (necessarily!) by the emergence of Jesus' resurrection in your own life?

27. We may ask formally that if God's exaltation of Jesus affirms his act of humbly emptying himself to be the form of fullest divine revelation, what are the implications of this "kenoticism" (self-emptying) for the Christian understanding of the very nature of God?

    That is, if the Hymn to Christ of Phil 2:6–11 truly reveals God's very own nature, then the twin phases of Jesus' Coming, in self-humiliation even unto death, and divine affirmation through exaltation, have enormous consequences. Try to think through these consequences, and how they might impact our very lives as Christians, "in Christ Jesus" (Phil 2:5). See especially Phil 2:1–5, 12–13.

---

5. Jüngel, "Emergence," 35–58.

Part Four (Session 8)

Growing into the Fullness of God's Life

The Catechism Continues

As well as drawing direct consequences from baptismal texts, the NT catechetical scheme functions via another set of ideas: "flesh" versus "Spirit."

- **Gal 5:16-25** (the next session lays the foundation for Gal 5) and **Rom 8:1-16** use the schema of *old* sinful nature or "flesh" vs. *new* human nature in the "Spirit," and the implications of these two spheres of existence. Recall figures 2, 3, and 5.

- **Rom 6:1-18** and **Col 2:11-15** (2:16—3:14) speak directly of "baptism" (referring to the complex of water rite and the Holy Sprit) and its immediate consequences. (And see too 1 **Cor 12:12-13**, comparing 1 Cor 10:1-4; Gal 3:27-28; and Eph 2:5-6.)

Continuing the Catechism's Sections

V   **John 15:18—16:11; 16:18-24, 33** are classic passages regarding the opposition of "the world" to the Gospel and the conflict it provokes. Jesus in the Garden of Gethsemane is surely the climax, albeit in a curious form—**Mark 14:32-41**.

Part Four (Session 8): Growing into the Fullness of God's Life

As the Lord's Prayer itself would suggest ("save us from the time of trial and deliver us from the Evil One"), the birth pangs of the messianic age are a basic given in the scheme of things. Yahweh's war against "all that is proud and lifted up" (Isa 2:12, remember session 1), from "the floods [that] lift up their voice" (Ps 93:3) to "Rahab [being/needing to be] cut to pieces" (Isa 51:9; Ps 89:10) via humanity's nigh inevitable "forgetfulness," "perversity," and "haughty eyes" (Deut 8:11, 14, 32:20; Prov 6:17)—this war reaches its climax with the arrival of Jesus on stage. Indeed, the opening chapters of Mark's Gospel (1–3) would suggest Jesus *deliberately provokes* the conflict. This is largely true: God's coming to (re)claim the world and (re)establish the divine rule among people and over the cosmos *will meet* with an essential opposition—given the way things are. The Markan Way of the Cross, which is Jesus' "mysterious" Way of the kingdom of God, is to a large degree determined precisely by such opposition. See especially **Mark 8:31, 9:31, and 10:33–34**. Yet what does God make of this conflict that Jesus' Coming provokes?

Such is the wisdom and power of God (echoes of 1 Cor 1–2) that even this very *rejection* is turned around, *both* to God's glory *and* to humanity's redemption; the human and cosmic denial of God's ways and ends becomes in God's Way the very fulfilment of his eternal Purpose and End; the human and cosmic defiant "No!" to God is in Christ Jesus itself denied by the divine "Yes!" or affirmation of this very human creature. This is the wonder of the breadth, length, height, and depth of God's love in Christ Jesus. Little wonder then that Paul concludes as he does in Rom 11:33–36! Little wonder, too, that he insists immediately afterwards upon Christians "not being conformed to this aeon, but being transformed by the renewing of [their] minds" (Rom 12:2). For this age is characterised by a fundamental idolatrous and antagonistic cast of mind, resulting in sin's due "reward" in disorder and death. (We should note the exegetical link, via worship, between the start of Rom 1:16–32, and this new start in Rom 12:1–2.) But God determines his human creature to *life*, to the Image of the One from Heaven, who is Life-giving Spirit (John 3:16; 1 Cor 15:45–49). *In faithful knowledge of* this *calling*, the church's membership is summoned to stand and withstand the wiles of the Evil One with due watchfulness and prayer. But there is ever only one way that Christians *may* "stand"—through the power of the Cross. This is genuine Christian discipleship, following in the Way of the Master.

VI   Therefore, put on the full armor of God, so that when the day of evil comes, you may be able to stand your ground, and after you have done everything, to stand. (Eph 6:13 NRSV)

From the earliest of Paul's letters, 1 Thess 5:1–11, to near the last, **Eph 6:10–18**, which is the fullest exposition of our catechetical form, via the likes of **Rom 13:11–14**, we have this common theme of *warfare*, which expresses the Christian's spiritual power and authority "in Christ Jesus." But not only does Paul expressly teach it; *he powerfully embodies it* (**2 Cor 2:14—6:13**).[1] When he says (Phil 3:10–11), "In order that I may know Christ and the power of his resurrection and the fellowship of his sufferings, being conformed to his death, if somehow I may attain the resurrection from the dead," this is no idle mystical speculation. It is grounded profoundly in his experience of having the treasure of the Gospel's revelation in the clay vessel of his human frame (see too Gal 1:16, "*in* me")—yet knowing too the deliverance of God in just *this* frame (see **2 Cor 1:3–11, 4:7–12**).

Paul's bold declaration to "imitate me" is based on his own performance of a near absolute imitation of Christ. His life has become conformed to the Master whose disciple he is. For his own sense of the truth of the Gospel is in his own "imitation of Christ," which he then seeks to "pass on" to the Corinthian Church in *their* imitation of *him* (**1 Cor 10:33**, Καθὼς κἀγώ/*kathōs* kagō: **11:1–2; 11:23, 15:3**). In this way, his apostolic authority is embedded in his own concrete knowledge of *the torah's having been written upon his own heart by the Holy Spirit*, which in turn grants him the freedom to offer this very life-transforming power to others under God (2

---

1. For two texts that address this vital NT feature of Gospel ministry, see Hafemann, *Suffering and Ministry*, and Young and Ford, *Meaning and Truth*.

PART FOUR (SESSION 8): GROWING INTO THE FULLNESS OF GOD'S LIFE

Cor 3–4, paraphrased). For Paul, the authority of the Gospel is a veritable form of grace imbued life. Yet a form of life whose criterion is ever and only the Word of the Cross: "*Crux probat omnia!*", as Martin Luther says.[2] And under the sign of this Cross, Christians may supremely prevail by means of the fulsome armamentarium with which the exalted Christ equips them (Eph 6:10–17)! Just so is "this aeon/the world" under "crisis"/judgment, with its "rulers and authorities disarmed," "stripped of their power" (Col 2:15), and the Christian "under the mercy."

Summary—To Repeat

The two prayers of Ephesians (1:15–23 and 3:14–21) are especially appropriate when seen in the context of the NT catechism. For they speak of our need *to realize* who we *are* "in Christ Jesus."

- ▶ The first invites to *see and understand/come to know* the reality into which/whom Christians have been immersed;
- ▶ The second declares the need for all this to be *cashed out*, to be *put into effect*, and so to *become a living reality*.

In other words, the English word "realize" has uniquely this double sense to it. *Just so, we are to* become *in the Holy Spirit who we* are *in Christ Jesus*. Selwyn's six sections of the baptismal catechism unpack the various features involved in this realization of the economy of the triune God among us, of the significance of who Jesus is and what he has accomplished "for us and for our salvation" in the power of the Holy Spirit. This is what God has made (of) us! All the rest is but "Yes" and "Amen" (2 Cor 1:20)— that is, our own "acknowledgement, recognition, and confession" (so Karl Barth's threefold description of faith) of the Glory of the

---

2. *Crux probat omnia*: the cross is the criterion for evaluating everything. See McGrath, *Luther's Theology*, 219, especially note 42, which references Moltmann's *The Crucified God* but in the German original, of which the subtitle more forcefully uses the twin words *Grund und Kritik*, the latter being better translated as "criterion" rather than "criticism" as in the official English translation (1974).

triune God, who transfers us out of darkness into his own marvelous light (Col 1:12–14).

> ### Questions for Reflection
>
> 28. The Summary Chart in Appendix 4 shows how the NT catechism makes use of grammar to make a theological point or series of points. What has been done for us and to us "in Christ Jesus" is indicated by means of verbs in the past tense, the indicative mood and the passive voice: "you have been." Parallel to such expressions are verbs in the present imperative active. Together, the complete schema is as follows, for example: since you have been crucified with Christ Jesus, now therefore put off/abstain/put to death! Since you have been co-raised with Christ Jesus, put on/walk in newness of life!
>
> 29. One way of cultivating the means for realizing these sets of verbs and thereafter the entire schema in your life is to trawl through the Epistles and *draw up a chart of contrasting pairs*: Adam/Christ, wages of sin/free gift of God, death/eternal life, flesh/Spirit, law/grace or promise, darkness/light, idols/living and true God, man of dust/man from heaven, etc. In this Way and only in this Way—of dying and rising—is the image of God restored in us humans.

Part Five (Session 9)

God's Faithfulness in Overflowing Life

Our final session will give one example of how all this works, of how living with the triune God may be traced during a complex exegetical exercise such as Paul undertakes here. It also links directly with what we've seen in Part 1 earlier, and the subsequent fulfillment of the OT in the NT with Jesus, Parts 2 and 3. Herewith therefore **Gal 3:1—4:7**.

We may recall the story of God's dealings with people takes on specific focus with the call of Abram/Abraham, the ancestor of the Israelite nation.

Gen 12:1-3	God promises three things to Abram: land, descendants, blessing

The entire OT story circles around these three: *Will* there be descendants? Will they live in the land—or not? Will they be *blessed* there—or not? Will *they be* a blessing? Or will the land "vomit them out" (Leviticus)? Will a remnant then return, perhaps? A raft of such permutations drives the story. . . . It is this covenant promise, furthermore, which gives the Israelites a keen sense of *history*. They have a *destiny*, since they have a *destination*, a goal.

Yet this goal turns out to be rather curious, even mysterious. For in order to fulfil the Covenant, in the end, God himself comes and enacts the part of the *human* partner in the Covenant. Jesus is *the* anointed Israelite before Israel's God, Yahweh, whom Jesus calls "Abba! Father!" and whose mission Jesus the Messiah, the true Son, faithfully fulfills through the power of the Holy Spirit. (The easiest NT representation of this idea is **John 15:1**, "I am the true vine and my Father is the gardener." The vine is a classic OT symbol for Israel: see **Ps 80**, especially vv. 8–13, and **Isa 5:1–7**.)[1] Our own participation in this fulfillment has been carefully lain out in previous sessions. Now, however, we conclude this series by explicitly couching this fulfillment in trinitarian terms, using Paul's explanation of it in one of his earliest letters.

To our twenty-first century ears, Paul's argument is at times rather tight and even strange. Yet, to the fore is Paul's attempt to explain, by means of a judicious use of authoritative Scriptures, that not only has this faithful Jew, Jesus, brought about the fulfillment of the Abrahamic Covenant for the sake of the Jews, but also for the sake of the Gentiles as well. And his reasoning is simply this: *all along* "the nations"/"Gentiles" were signalled as heirs to the promise in the Genesis story. But to get there, Paul has to weave a veritable tapestry of text and commentary in vv. 6–18, contrasting not exactly the failure of folks to live up to the commands of the law, but rather the failure of the Law itself to deliver what only the Promise would deliver, *the fullness of eschatological life.*

Verses 1–5 of chapter 3 are an opening gambit, contrasting performing "works of the law" with "hearing the message with faith/faith-hearing the Gospel message" as the means of "receiving the Spirit" and all that the Spirit brings. (See too Rom 3:27—4:5. Note, "your reward," *misthos* in the LXX of Gen 15:1, is the very word Paul takes up in Rom 4:4, "wages.")

---

1. See too Hays, *Reading Backwards,* and Hays, *Echoes of Scripture,* where he details how the four Evangelists all tell in their respective ways the story of Jesus as a retelling of the story of Israel, which Jesus fulfills and even transcends, since he is simultaneously both the perfect human covenant partner and "somehow" the Covenant God, Yahweh, embodied. Note also, in the context of this "simultaneously both", Jenson, *ST 1,* Chapter Five, "The Persons of God's Identity", 75–89, where he begins the kinds of theological moves that will establish Trinitarian speech—of Jesus the Israelite who represents *both* the community of Israel before Yahweh, serving Israel and Yahweh, *and* Yahweh to Israel. See again *LDL,* chapters 3–5 for something of how all this works, taking up some key NT texts.

Then in the next section, **verses 6–9**, Paul first quotes **Gen 15:6** almost verbatim. Then he moves in v. 7 to announce, "You know then that those of faith, these are 'sons of Abraham.'" How so? Verse 8 combines **Gen 12:3** and **Gen 22:18** (with an echo of **Gen 18:18** as well). But we must notice the key to Paul's position: it is *"in* you (singular)," that is Abraham, that God "blesses the Gentiles"—Abraham is acting in the role of a *representative*—which "blessing" is then to be equated with "justification" in the first part of the verse, the notion with which we started in v. 6. All of this is rooted in the authority of "Scripture" itself which "pre-preaches [this] Gospel," corroborating their Spirit-faith-experience. The result, v. 9, is that all "those of faith" are blessed "along with the believing Abraham."

Verses 10–14 figure a number of contrasting motifs: law vs. faith, curse vs. blessing. These verses have furthermore been the generator of the venerable Lutheran Tradition, that the Law's job is to convict the sinner, since no one is *ever capable* of fulfilling *"all* the works of the Law": QED, only faith may save us. The problem, however, is whether this interpretation, as hallowed as it may be, is what Paul actually means here. For who exactly is Paul referring to with the expression, "the Just One of Faith," from **Hab 2:4**? True, not those who live by the Law, as Paul himself was previously doing (**Phil 3:6**), which form of righteousness was even then "blameless," as he saw it! Rather, even though **Lev 18:5** speaks of a form of life through the Law, **Deut 27:26**, which Paul brings to bear in v. 10, specifically announces a curse upon both observant and unobservant law-keepers alike—simply because the Law *per se* does not have its origin in faith (v. 12a), and only "the Just One of Faith" (whoever that is) "will live" (v. 11b)!

And who is this person? "The Righteous One" is almost certainly a messianic title in first century Judaism, and is so applied to Jesus in Acts 3:14, 7:52, 22:14; 1 Pet 3:18; and 1 John 2:1. Moreover, this One acts *as the people's representative*, much as Abraham is back in v. 8; but most curiously, the form this representation takes is by absorbing now (v. 13) the "curse" of the Law—following **Deut 21:23**—the curse-bearing role of which may be seen to "redeem us," setting us free as slaves are redeemed. This pattern of exchange is found expressly in **2 Cor 5:21**, and the expression "become for us" is repeated in 1 Cor 1:30 as well. And the reason for/the consequence of this exchange then follows in verse 14.

The two consecutive clauses are in parallel, interpreting one another:

- so that *the blessing of Abraham* might come to the Gentiles in Christ Jesus,
- so that *the promise of the Spirit* we might receive through faith.

From the tight parallelism of Paul's construction, we can readily see that "the blessing of Abraham" (see Gen 28:4) is to be equated with "the promise of the Spirit"; the classic expression "in Christ Jesus" (as the Messianic representative of Israel) equals "through faith"; and *both* Gentiles *and* Jews are now on an equal footing before God (see too Eph 1:12-13, 2:11-19)—thanks to Jesus the Messiah's Coming; Gentile "sinners"/"outsiders" are now "brought near" in the Messiah, who fulfills God's Covenant with Abraham for/on behalf of both groups.

Verses 15-22 then finish off this part of Paul's argument. As I say, the detail of v. 16, with Paul's emphasis upon "the seed (singular) of Abraham," might sound odd to our ears, but it parallels exactly the kind of expression found also in 2 Sam 7:12-14. Once more, the Messiah was himself designated "the seed of David"; so it is easy for Paul, a rabbinically trained Jew, to so argue the same of Gen 17:7, (perhaps 18:18), and 22:18, namely that *all the "inherited"* (v. 18) *promises of God to Abraham coalesce in the One Singular Descendant*, the Messiah of Israel, the Just One, who himself lives by faith.

Conclusion

Paul has woven many threads together during this intricate argument of Gal 3:1-22. Not all of them have been addressed here, nor have those mentioned been treated equally. Rather, our point is to highlight *the trinitarian suggestions* that Paul makes, while he

PART FIVE (SESSION 9): GOD'S FAITHFULNESS IN OVERFLOWING LIFE

proceeds to lay down his reasons for seeing the Abrahamic Covenant's blessings as coming upon all those who are "in Christ Jesus," who, as *the* Seed of Abraham, was ever destined to inherit the promises of God to bless Abraham and "all the families of the earth" before him. Vital now to this inheritance, this promise of blessing, is the Gift of the Holy Spirit *himself* (see the parallel in **Isa 44:3**, as well as Gal 3:14). That is, *previously* **1 Kgs 4:20-25** presented the fulfillment of the Abrahamic covenant with the Israelites settled in their land and blessed (see session 1);[2] *now* the picture is genuinely global, with its fulfillment embracing all peoples able to inherit the Spirit of God—who clearly transcends as Creator any bounded territory.[3] (The global scope of the Gospel beyond the limitations of given geography is also affirmed in Jesus' conversation with the Samaritan woman, **John 4:19-24**.)

Furthermore, we may *infer* from this section of Galatians *the pattern or sequence of Giver-Gift-Recipient*, our model of GGR, of the Father giving the Holy Spirit to the Son, who receives the fullness of God's Inheritance—God himself! Yet not simply for himself but on behalf of "all humankind" (v. 22), who "have been imprisoned under sin," "in order that" (the crucial consecutive conjunction again) "the promise, through the faith(fulness) of Jesus Christ, might be given to those who believe." For this "Just One" is now *not alone* in *this* Inheritance; *others* share his destiny. **Gal 3:25-29** is very explicit. *All those* who are "put into Christ Jesus"—the baptismal language is strongly to the fore—are one in Christ and so heir to the promise, *together with him*.

---

2. For those who wish to examine this vital feature of the OT, see Brueggemann, *Land*; Habel, *Land is Mine*; Wright, *God's People*; and Janzen, "Land," 143–54. How all this might be transposed under the New Covenant in Jesus and the Holy Spirit cannot be pursued here—despite its evident importance in our twenty-first century with its environmental concerns. For another day!

3. See Janzen's conclusion, "Land," 153: "It means to recognize the potential of all lands and places—of the whole ecosystem [and we might add necessarily, of all peoples therefore]—to be chosen by the transcendent God of the Bible to work signs of his election and presence."

Concluding Section

The last verses of the entire section, 4:1–7, reinforce this conclusion. Paul is almost certainly relying on an early Christian creedal formula here, which he puts to his own use. He is also assuming a powerful metaphor, that of the Roman legal practice of a child's legally coming of age (around 12–14, but also up to 20 if the father so decreed). This meant they are under custodians prior to that and are as good as any slave in the father's household, being still a legal minor. We pick it up at v. 4 (own translation):

- But when the fullness of the time came: the idea of fulfillment is often found explicitly in Matthew and especially at Mark 1:15. It is of course key to the entire NT.
- God sent forth his Son: this includes a typical "sending formula," as found elsewhere in Paul and John (Rom 8:3, John 10:36, 17:3, 18:37b), and while it need not imply the Son's pre-existence, it probably does in Paul's hands.
- Born/becoming of a woman, born/becoming under the Law: i.e., a true human being and the One who faithfully submitted to the Law's yoke, duly fulfilling his mission thereby—which was . . .
- In order that those under the Law he might redeem: the first consecutive clause—an exact replica of 3:14—this time continuing the redemption from slavery metaphor, both of Gentiles who are under their "elemental spirits," and of Jews who are under their Law's "custodianship"—all this the first goal/result/purpose of the Son's being sent;
- In order that the adoption of sonship *we* might receive: the second consecutive clause and the high point of Paul's argument, *the end goal* of it all indeed . . .
- And because *you* are sons, God sent forth the Spirit of his Son . . . which goal is demonstrated and effected by the self-same Spirit the Son bears, who now . . .

PART FIVE (SESSION 9): GOD'S FAITHFULNESS IN OVERFLOWING LIFE

- Into *our* hearts, crying, "Abba! Father!": the fact that the formula still uses the Aramaic word for "Dad," which is supremely found on Jesus' lips in the Gospels, is highly significant. See too Rom 8:15-16, 23; Eph 1:5.
- So, you are no more a slave but a son: the great transition (albeit in metaphor)!
- And if a son, also an heir through God: because of adoption into *the* Son and heir, so too now are *we* "heirs of all things" *together with* Jesus. All of which is God's doing.
- We might note finally the order of things. In the larger context of his argument, Paul has reasoned from his converts' reception of the Spirit (3:2-5, 14b) to their being "sons of God" (3:26), which is also the order of his presentation in Rom 8:15-17. Here in 4:4-6, however, that relationship seems to be reversed by saying, "Because you are sons, God sent the Spirit of his Son into our hearts." The debate as to whether the proper order is first sonship and then the gift of the Spirit, or first the reception of the Spirit and then sonship, has been fervent and heated. Yet perhaps it is only the case that Paul is using a preestablished formula here, while in any case elsewhere (Rom 8:1-2, 9-11) he shows just *how intimately connected each is to the other*. Just so, God's ways with us are ever and only by means of the Son and the Spirit, in the power of the Spirit and through the Son, who together enable us *to participate in the eternal dynamic of giving and receiving* unto the Father's glory and praise and honor. Amen; even so be it!
- "The purpose of the Son's mission was to give the rights of sonship; the purpose of the Spirit's mission, to give the power of using them" (Henry Barclay Swete, *The Holy Spirit in the New Testament*). Or Heinrich Schlier, *Der Brief an die Galater*: "God bestows on us not only the status of sons [through the sending of his Son] but also the character and knowledge of sons [through the sending of the Spirit]. And he bestows on us the

character and knowledge of sons because we are already in the status of sons."[4]

- As well as being part of an early Christian formula, vv. 4–6 display key features of a wider, richer narrative, and linking with 3:13–14 (another formula), trace how it is that Paul can argue the way he does. Behind 3:1—4:7 as a whole lies the Grand Christian Story, which protrudes at key points via these two formulae, to reinforce and justify his presentation now to these Galatian Christians.[5] Just so, the doctrine of the Trinity summarizes the basic character in the theodrama—Father, Son, and Holy Spirit—whose acts *are* the one economy of human and cosmic salvation.

- A final piece of historical theology. Down the centuries there has been no small debate surrounding how the Old and New Testaments tie together. Lutheran and Reformed types in particular lock horns over the number of covenants, and their role(s) and fulfillment(s): are there two "dispensations" or one? 2 Cor 3:6–11 shows there are in fact two, while Gal 3:1—4:7 also shows how the singular Just One, who himself lives by faith, enacts and fulfills *all* the OT covenants, *both* the Abrahamic *and* the Mosaic, and therewith their Davidic formulations, simultaneously in his own unique mission—coalescing them all even in himself, the *autobasileia* (Origen) in person![6] See again "A Covenant Summary," pages 75–83.

---

4. Both quotes are from Bruce, *Epistle to the Galatians*, 198.

5. See Hays, *Faith of Jesus Christ*, for a thoroughgoing treatment of this idea.

6 See also Jenson, *ST 1*, 69, for how, despite their vital contrasts, "the dynastic contract [necessarily coheres] with desert torah ... as an eschatological promise," of how "Davidic and [Mosaic] covenants come together after all" at the End, in "righteousness and justice", in "steadfast love and faithfulness", those four foundational covenant terms (so for example Pss 89:14, 97:2, 25:10, 72:1–2, Exod 34:6–7).

PART FIVE (SESSION 9): GOD'S FAITHFULNESS IN OVERFLOWING LIFE

A Final Reflection

30. How then might we place ourselves more fully into the "receptive" mode, to receive more readily the Gift the Father has for his sons and daughters in Christ Jesus? Part of the answer lies in the form of Andrei Rublev's icon of the Three Angels (based on Gen 18, a favorite of the early church) painted c. 1410 (see below). For at its base is a deliberate gap between the feet, inviting the viewer to enter into the circle formed by the turning heads and the flow of bodies and the feet. And of course, *where* one enters is the place of worship dominated by the Eucharistic cup of salvation! Just so, are we invited to participate in this circle of mutual giving and receiving among the Trinitarian persons, into the embrace of God's holy loving hospitality, in worshipful contemplation and adoration, which is the due human reflection (**2 Cor 3:18**) of that fullness of trinitarian "mutual regard" (Aquinas) that bathes in "the radiance" of each person's "supreme light" (Richard of St. Victor), "the delirium of arrival" (Milbank), in whose "embrace a host is a guest and a guest is a host" (Volf)—a veritable "perichoretic dance" (Fiddes), a sustained, convivial "conversational fugue" (Jenson).

    And so, enveloped by this triune God, whose perichoretic nature generates such humility and such glory among the Godhead that there's even room for us humans within that life and love, that freedom and light, may your own worship and adoration find other avenues of expression too, ones that might employ the musical, the visual arts, the poetic, "acts of mercy"—whatever conforms with your own gifts. For returning such gifts, offering them back with added interest to the Giver and Fount of All is the joyous point of it all. Amen; even so be it!

Andrei Rublev's icon of the Three Angels of Mamre, 1410

Conclusion

LIVING WITH THE TRIUNE God, Father, Son, and Holy Spirit, may indeed begin with the invocation of the threefold name at baptism.[1] Yet, thereafter, that Life itself is maintained by the judicious realization of the fullness of that baptismal existence and inheritance. This realization, too, has a twofold sense, as we've seen, by means of the likes of the two prayers in Ephesians: to be seen and understood, and so coming to know, as well as being put into effect or cashed out. Essentially, all the moves of the NT catechetical form are dependent upon one thing: our being put into Christ Jesus, the Incarnate One, humanity's representative and substitute, by being immersed in the Holy Spirit. For Jesus baptizes Christians into himself, his Body, with/by the Holy Spirit. Moreover, since Jesus' identity is also that of the divine Recipient according to GGR (see *LDL* for the account of this model, its justification, and elaboration), so Christians too may be viewed as mini-recipients "in him," in union with Christ.[2] As the start of chapter 9 of *LDL* puts it (page 151):

> This translates directly into the life of the church and into the lives of Christian disciples on the analogy of St. Paul's notion of "adoption." Just as humans become adopted sons and daughters of the Living God, through and in *the*

---

1. For this initial stance, see chapter 1, "Invocation: Trinity and Salvation," in Vickers, *Invocation and Assent*, 1–28, together with the introduction, xii-xiii; and more fully, Jenson, *ST*, 1.

2. From among the extensive literature on this key expression, see only Billings, *Union with Christ*.

Son, Jesus, crying "Abba! Father!" in the Holy Spirit, so too do we humans become recipients in *the* Recipient, becoming participants in the triune life of GGR. We humans are caught up into/baptized into the very "reiterative event" that *is* the triune God, sharing in the eternal "movement" of the Father's giving the Holy Spirit to the Son, etc. Nor is this understanding of Paul's unique. The conclusion we drew from our brief examination of the Fourth Gospel's Prologue in chapter 4, "More dots and some colors," follows a similar line of interpretation: "the Glory of the Father is . . . the begetting of many additional sons and daughters (τέκνα/*tekna*/children) from among humanity, through *the* Son (υἱός/*huios*), Jesus, and the gift of the Holy Spirit." One last observation: just as individual men and women, girls and boys, together become members of the Household of God, together are members of God's family, so too are individuals recipients together in the *totus Christus*, the Whole Christ, *the* Recipient. And extending this observation to combine Paul and John, we may say that Jesus is *the* Temple Recipient (John 1:14, 2:19–22), *the abode* of the immeasurable Gift of the Holy Spirit (John 3:34) from the Father, the Giver, who builds Christians together into the triune God's true dwelling place, *the* divine Home, through Jesus and in the Holy Spirit (1 Cor 3:16–17, Eph 1:15–23, 2:11–22, 4:7–16, 1 Pet 2:4–10).[3]

One last thing. As session 5 earlier explained, what the rite of baptism initiates, the Eucharistic rite continues or maintains—and rightly so. Since all is gracious gift, gratitude is the only due response.[4] But only as the Eucharist too is viewed in its appropriate fullness. For as chapter 8 of *LDL* spelled out, and session 5 signaled,

---

3. See again Beale, The Temple and the Church's Mission, notably chapters 12 and 13, "Theological Conclusions: the physical temple as a foreshadowing of God's and Christ's presence as the true temple," and "Practical reflections on Eden and the temple for the church in the twenty-first century."

4. As Barth expresses it, "χάρις (*charis*) always demands the answer of εὐχαριστία (*eucharistia*). Grace and gratitude belong together like heaven and earth. Grace evokes gratitude like the voice an echo. Gratitude follows grace like thunder lightening." *CD IV/1*, 41.

notably through the T. F. Torrance quote, *both* sacraments must be duly enveloped *within* the dynamic "field" that *is* the Holy Trinity—the envelopment of which is better appreciated by means of the model of GGR. Just so, the model of GGR may better come to life in the imaginations and lives of Christian disciples through their being "led by the hand" of Jesus, the Living Word himself, who supremely guides his flock by means of his voice attested in the Scriptures of the Old and New Testaments, and his writing *torah* on human hearts by the Spirit (John 10:3, 27–28, 20:16 [Jer 23:1–8; Ezek 34]; 2 Cor 3:1—4:6 [Jer 31:31–34; Ezek 36:22–28]). This workbook, we trust, has displayed something of the full scope of this theodrama, during which God has revealed and demonstrated his triune identity—that Name which is to be hallowed by all and known especially by those creatures in the divine image, who may graciously call him "Father" through the Son, Jesus, in the Holy Spirit.[5]

Concluding Reflection

31. "Beginning again at the beginning" (Karl Barth). We can reappropriate this description of Barth's of the theologian's task by applying it now to our own constant realization of one's glorious inheritance of the fullness of baptism into Christ Jesus by the Spirit, thus *becoming* who we *are*. What do you make of this depiction of Christian discipleship? How might we develop more fully the means both individually and corporately of realizing this form of discipleship? A key part of the answer is given in this workbook as being via the NT catechism; and so what do you make of this answer?

---

5. See especially *LDL*, page 88, question 14; and page 168, question 27 (among others).

A Closing Prayer
(Karl Barth, 1886–1968)

Lord our God, you have humbled yourself, that we may be exalted. You became poor, that we may become rich. You came to us, that we may come to you. You became a human being like us, that we may be drawn into participation in your eternal life: All of this from your free, undeserved grace; all of this in your dear Son, our Lord and Savior, Jesus Christ.

We are gathered here, in view of this mystery and wonder, to pray to you, praise you, and to proclaim and hear your Word. But we know that we cannot do these things under our own power, that it is you who free us to lift our hearts and thoughts to you. So we ask you to come now into our midst! Show us and open to us the path to you through your Holy Spirit, so that we may see with our own eyes your light that has come into the world, in order that our lives may indeed be witnesses to you. Amen.[1]

1. Barth, *Fifty Prayers*, 9.

Notes for Leaders

Introduction: This workbook is arranged in Five Parts and 9 Sessions. In effect, the sessions are pretty well chapters. Yet they are called "sessions" to emphasize the working nature of the material, as well as to suggest groups might like to work through the book together; certainly, the questions are designed as group discussion starters. If the latter, then it may very well take more than one actual session to cover off any one "chapter." For example, with session 6 on Ephesians a group might like to apportion a meeting for each of the three chapters, 1–3. However, as suggested below with the likes of session 2, in some cases, prolonging the study of the material on offer could detract from the main point of the session(s). How long therefore any particular group takes to complete the entire workbook will depend on its makeup; nor should this bother any of a group's members, who can surely work it out together. Enjoy; and may you be blessed!

Part One: These opening sessions are a bit of a romp, so prepare well beforehand and time yourself carefully. *Read out loud* all those passages in **bold type**—though naturally the other references are given for you to enjoy too, just as you may very well have to select which major motif passages to read out loud in Session 2. Three ideas suggest what it is we are seeking here and what *not*. (1) It is a broad-stroke overview, like a rapidly drawn cartoon, rather than a fine etching. (2) Just as children in a kindergarten are asked "to join up the dots/follow the numbers," so this is what those passages given here are doing. We are not asked, however, "to color in our picture" when we've outlined it. This would take us far too long! (3) The "basic analogy" of Part Two, which ties together the Old and New Testaments (see under Questions for Reflection, number 9) may be invoked here if questions arise at this point. What we are not doing, however, is examining all these OT pieces in detail, nor how they in fact relate to the NT (which is a debated, academic question, initiated by Gabler's famous lecture of 1787 and still being reformulated deeply today). It is just the *principle* we are trying to get across—that Jesus ties up the OT by fulfilling it, and then offers us a share in this fulfillment. Indeed, the NT is the story of how God the Author writes *himself* into human history, becoming the unique actor in the drama. To sum up: the basic theme is that of *promise and fulfillment*, and how this results in our own *destiny*—which we can and should choose and affirm through faith in Jesus Christ.

If you want to make a PowerPoint of the diagrams, it may be helpful. Color Israelite history/Old brown (for earthy), Day of Yahweh, and lines D1 and D2, red (a warning type color), and the Messianic Age/New blue (for royalty).

Part Two: While there is much we could focus on in this third session—there are, after all, four Gospels given us, each with their respective narrative renderings of Jesus—the point is to see as clearly as possible the unexpected, even scandalous Way Jesus brings in the Father's Glorious Rule among us. This lays the foundations for what is to come in further sessions, as we learn to share in God's own Story, God's own Life, through Jesus and in the Holy Spirit.

Part Three: These two sessions unpack how people are immersed in(to) the Life of God and may remain in this triune Life. The three legged stool of Christian initiation undergirds all else. Nor should folk get especially hung-up on the three labels I have used to dramatically express the nature of each of the legs. As with many things, we are dealing here with tendencies taken to extremes. For all that, the labels have proven helpful in showing people where they have gaps in their appreciation of both Church history, and Christian understanding and experience. Thereafter, the point is to have these gaps filled, to strengthen our Christian experience.

Part Four: In your preparation before this first session 6 it may help to use a commentary on Ephesians. For all that, however, as with sessions 1 and 2, the point is not to go into every conceivable detail but to have before us *God's Grand Design*, and especially Paul's *two key prayers*. (One twin element of this Design does stand out: *King David* captured Jerusalem, making it his capital and providing for the *Temple* to be built there [2 Sam 5 and 1 Chr 28–29]. This Royal Zion theology of the OT then finds extraordinary fulfillment in this NT letter, as you will see). *The aim* is to gain an impression of the sheer immensity of God's gracious purposes—and *our own inclusion in them*. Yes, even little old you and me! So try to keep the conversation quite personal, noting the use of "us"/"we"/"you" in the text (probably, by the way, originally references to "we" Jews and "you" Gentiles, but susceptible now to being reapplied). In other words, there is little room for what some folk seem to enjoy: a privatized religion that focuses upon "individual salvation" as "life insurance after one dies." Rather, the vision is *both* personal *and* cosmic, all at once, *both* now *and* forever. One local analogy from New Zealand sees this glorious inclusion of various folk, both individual and tribal or national, in God's great economy of grace, as being akin to the intricate braided rivers of the South Island: there's a single source (Eph 3:14), yet the various channels downstream weave their interlocking paths through the gravel, until all finally reach the sea at the river's mouth to become immersed in the vast ocean (the *totus Christus* as described in the two prayers and their fulfillment).

Sessions 7 and 8 unpack the reconstructed NT catechism as put together by E. G. Selwyn in his commentary of 1 Peter written in 1947. There he detailed extensively, in a 100-page appendix, the interrelation of 1 Peter and other NT epistles via this NT "form of teaching." Not only does he demonstrate with great skill and patience these intricate NT links; *he also offers a profound way of "reading" Scripture and practicing the Faith*. In a nutshell, when we/you "read" Holy Scripture, look for two things: What God has done for us/you, on y/our behalf, and thereafter to you and in you, "in Christ Jesus" via the Holy Spirit. Then, secondly, by careful

Notes for Leaders

"attention" (Simone Weil/Karl Barth) to these things, may you/we learn to "recycle" all that gracious activity, "to realize" it—where "realize" means (1) to see and understand/come to know (Eph 1:15–23), and (2) to put into effect/cash out (Eph 3:14–21), i.e., look for the realization of the triune God's answers to these two prayers in and through you/us! If the group needs to spend more time on this material than can be covered in two sessions, so be it.

Part Five: This final session offers an exegetical reading of Gal 3:1—4:7. This section of an early letter of Paul's is selected as it ties together well all the previous sessions, offering, too, an example of how the trinitarian model of GGR lies embedded within a fulsome theological presentation of the Gospel of Jesus, unveiling as well how folk might thus live with(in) the triune God of the Gospel.

A Covenant Summary

A. Again and again in the OT, but especially in Jeremiah and Ezekiel, there's this refrain: "You shall be my people and I will be your God." It reflects in a nutshell the covenant formula: there is this profound covenant relationship between Yahweh on the one hand and the people of Israel on the other.

Exod 6:6–8   So tell the Israelites that I say to them, "I am the LORD/Yahweh; I will rescue you and set you free from your slavery to the Egyptians. I will raise my mighty arm to bring terrible punishment upon them, and I will save you. I will make you my own people, and I will be your God. You will know that I am Yahweh your God when I set you free from slavery in Egypt. I will bring you to the land that I solemnly promised to give to Abraham, Isaac, and Jacob; and I will give it to you as your own possession. I am Yahweh." (GNT)

Jer 7:23   I gave them this command: "Obey my voice; and I will be your God, and you shall be my people. And walk in all the ways I command you, that it may go well with you." (NIV)

A Covenant Summary

Jer 11:2–5   Remind the people of Judah and Jerusalem about the terms of my covenant with them. Say to them, "This is what the LORD, the God of Israel, says: Cursed is anyone who does not obey the terms of my covenant! For I said to your ancestors when I brought them out of the iron-smelting furnace of Egypt, 'If you obey me and do whatever I command you, then you will be my people, and I will be your God.' I said this so I could keep my promise to your ancestors to give you a land flowing with milk and honey—the land you live in today." (NLT)

Ezek 34:30–31   In this way, they will realize that I am their LORD God, and am with them. And that they, the community of Israel, are my people, says the Sovereign LORD. You are my flock, you are the flock I tend; I am your God—so runs the oracle of the Lord Yahweh.

B. These few examples show two key things:[1]

1. God's *Promise* to the patriarchs—to Abraham, Isaac and Jacob. This takes the threefold form of land, descendants, and blessing; see Gen 12:1–3. The entire OT Story circles around these three, as we've seen: *will* there be descendants? *will* they live in the land—or *not*? will they be *blessed* there—or *not*? will they *be* a blessing? Or will the land "vomit them out" (Leviticus)? will a *remnant* then return—perhaps? A raft of such permutations drives the Story.

---

[1]. See Clements, *OT Theology*, who makes these two categories seminal. Naturally, the discipline of Old Testament Theology has burgeoned: see only Hasel, *OT Theology*, who brilliantly sets the scene, with subsequent offerings by the likes of Rolf Knierim, Walter Brueggemann, Paul House, Bruce Waltke, Walter Moberly, and John Goldingay.

A Covenant Summary

2. Then there's the succinct beginning to the Ten Commandments: "I am Yahweh your God, who brought you out of the land of Egypt, out of the land of slavery; you shall have no other gods besides me." Just as the Ten Commandments summarize the Law, so the *Torah*—to give it its proper Hebrew name: God's teaching or instructions for life—so the Torah expresses, in its fulness, the *kind* of relationship the people of Israel are to have, with Yahweh on the one hand and among themselves on the other.

C. As well as these two key covenant expressions, of Promise and of Torah, the OT uses four major *words* to characterize the covenant relationship between God and Israel:

1. *Hesed*: variously translated "mercy" or "grace" (KJV), "steadfast love" (NRSV/ESV), "love" (NIV)

2. ^{E}*met*: variously translated "faithfulness" (NRSV/NIV/ESV), "truth" (KJV), "constancy" (JB)

3. *Mispat*: translated as "justice" or "judgment," enacted by a *shophet* or "judge"

4. *Sedaqah/sedeq*: translated "righteousness" or "righteous" = conformity to a two-way relationship, i.e. the covenant itself.

Typically, the first two describe God himself, while the second two Israel's authentic response, especially among Israelites themselves. Yet the second pair also describe God's actions towards Israel or individual Israelites, arising from the covenant relationship. Again and again we see this in the Book of Psalms.

D. Yet there is a deep ambiguity, ambivalence even, to all this covenant material. We see it starkly in Deuteronomy, and thereafter in the history somewhat edited from this Deuteronomic perspective (1 & 2 Kings). *On the one hand*, God's covenant with Israel is purely *his election*:

> For you are a people holy to the LORD your God. The LORD your God has chosen you out of all the peoples on the face of the earth to be his people, his treasured

possession. The LORD did not set his affection on you and choose you because you were more numerous than other peoples, for you were the fewest of all peoples. But it was because the LORD loved you and kept the oath he swore to your forefathers that he brought you out with a mighty hand and redeemed you from the land of slavery, from the power of Pharaoh king of Egypt. Know therefore that the LORD your God is God; he is the faithful God, keeping his covenant of love to a thousand generations of those who love him and keep his commands. (Deut 7:6-9 NIV)

Then on the other hand, just as Moses declares all Yahweh's sovereign will and testament for the covenant people of God to *dwell in the land* and be *blessed*, in his third and final farewell speech (Deut 29-30) he predicts the inevitable *failure* of the people due to their *faithless response*. So what do we make of this *deep irony and paradox*:

- For how can it be that a people—who cannot keep covenant being such a "stiff-necked" (Deut 10:16) people, "who have eaten their fill and *forgotten*" (8:11-20)—should be given a land *on the express condition* that they do so keep covenant with Yahweh?
- where the possibilities of the ways of faith (in *remembering*, in obedience, in moral behavior, etc.) contrast so explicitly with the dismal actualities of *self-trust*?
- where "blessings and curses" (chapters 27 and 28) therefore represent not so much an either/or set of *consequences*—"therefore choose life!" (Deut 30:19)—as an inevitable *sequence* of first blessing, *followed then by* curse, followed by . . . the hope of restoration/recreation???!

This sequence works itself out painfully in the histories of first the house of Israel, who go into exile when Samaria is destroyed in 722 BC, and then the house of Judah, with their exile to Babylon at the start of the 6th century, Jerusalem itself finally being destroyed in 587 BC.

A Covenant Summary

And what of the hope of *full restoration* . . . ?

E. The answer is hinted at in Deut 30:6 (NB the chapter as a whole) and then found in Jeremiah 31:31–34, where God himself provides a *New Covenant*.

> Behold, the days are coming, declares the Lord, when I will make a new covenant with the house of Israel and the house of Judah, not like the covenant that I made with their fathers on the day when I took them by the hand to bring them out of the land of Egypt, my covenant that they broke, though I was their husband, declares the Lord. But this is the covenant that I will make with the house of Israel after those days, declares the Lord: I will put my law within them, and I will write it on their hearts. And I will become their God, and they shall become my people. And no longer shall each one teach his neighbor and each his brother, saying, "Know the Lord," for they shall all know me, from the least of them to the greatest, declares the Lord. For I will forgive their iniquity, and I will remember their sin no more. (ESV)

There are a number of key features to this renewal of the covenant relationship between Yahweh and his People:

1. "The days are coming/the time is coming, when I will make." God is looking into a future time when something new will take place, something that he himself will do. It is entirely *God's sovereign initiative*, wrought upon the People of God by God himself—and no other. Furthermore, as we see in the parallel version of this New Covenant in Ezekiel, the *reasons* for God's actions are also entirely his own (36:22–23): "It is not for your sake, O house of Israel, that I am about to act, but for the sake of my holy name, which you have profaned among the nations. I will sanctify my great name . . ." (Just so the first petition of the Lord's Prayer!)

2. Next, we can see that this renewing action of God has a twofold movement to it. With the characteristic covenant formula, "I will become their God, and they shall become

my people," God makes himself responsible for *both* ends of this movement. God says he will make himself the agent *both* for God becoming theirs *and* for their becoming God's own. Yet how does this happen? The answer is clear: only with and through and in Christ Jesus. For with the Coming of Jesus, God enacts, he embodies, this twofold movement. For in Jesus, God acts *towards us* as the Incarnate God on the one hand, but on the other hand he *also* acts on behalf of humanity, as the substitute and representative Human, *towards God*. With the Coming of Jesus, *God fulfills* both *poles of the covenant relationship*. He is Yahweh, the Father of Jesus, the One who calls and sends; *and* he is Jesus, Son of the Father, the true Vine and Servant of Israel, who responds in faithful obedience in the power of the Holy Spirit (Ps 80, Isa 5:1–7, Jn 15:1–17, Mk 1:11/Isa 42:1, Isa 61:1–3/Lk 4:14–30).[2]

3. Yet there is furthermore a twofold character to these two movements. The righteous grace of God in Christ Jesus has the twin elements of both judgment-and-mercy, mercy-and-judgment. God consigns all types of humanity to disobedience in order that he may have mercy on all types as Sin gets condemned in the flesh (so Rom 8:3 and notably 11:32, the climax of the entire argument, chapters 1–11). And both this disobedience and this mercy find their twin focus on Jesus, the "one and the same" (Chalcedonian Decree) human being—as the Crucified Messiah and Lamb of God, who bears the *curse* of the covenant on the tree for us (Gal 3:10–13, Acts 5:30,10:39, 1 Cor 1–4); and as the Resurrected Son of God, who enables the *blessings* of the covenant in the promised gift of the Holy Spirit to come on those who believe (Gal 3:14, Rom 1:4). Just so, John 1:29–34 in a nutshell, and

---

2. This twofold movement is the core of chapter 8, "Deconstruction," in *LDL*, which is heavily indebted to the work of T. F. Torrance. See also importantly, in the context of this simultaneity, Jenson, *ST 1, The Triune God*, Chapter Five, "The Persons of God's Identity," 75–89, where he begins the kinds of theological moves that will establish Trinitarian speech—of Jesus *the* Israelite Servant who represents *both* the community of Israel before Yahweh, serving Israel and Yahweh, *and* Yahweh to Israel.

A Covenant Summary

the other baptismal narratives (Mk 1:9–11, Matt 3:13–17, Lk 3:21–22, all of which echo Ps 2:7, Isa 42:1 & Gen 22:2).[3]

4. What the faithful Servant of Yahweh has accomplished on our behalf becomes ours too in faith, as we are incorporated/baptized into his entire mission—into his birth, life, death, resurrection and ascension—in the power and grace of the Holy Spirit. (See again those diagrams earlier.) And all this becomes ours as we are grafted into the Messiah (Rom 11:17–24), whose own Spirit writes God's *Torah* upon our hearts and minds (2 Cor 3:2–3), replacing our hearts of stone with lively hearts (Ezek 36:26–30), producing a harvest of love joy peace patience kindness goodness faithfulness meekness and self-control (Gal 5:22–23), whereby we too cry "Abba! Father!" (Gal 4:6, Rom 8:15) and "Jesus is Lord!" (1 Cor 12:3). The Renewed Covenant in both Jesus the Lord (Phil 2:6–11) and the Holy Spirit involves the intimate knowing of God as our Father, and ultimately our knowing as we are known (Gal 4:9, 1 Cor 13:12).[4]

F. What then of the relationship between Israel and the church? For both are clearly called the people of God. Briefly, we might say two extremes need to be avoided.

Firstly, we have the notion that the church has *superseded* Israel, that God has moved on from Israel to the church. Though it might be tempting to see this as the NT picture (and there are some suggestions this might be the case: e.g. the conclusion to the parable in Matt 21:41–44), overall the NT is more complex and subtle than this, as we must derive from the likes of 1 Peter 2:4–10 (which echoes the major text, Exod 19:3–6, as well as other scriptures) and Rom 9–11.

Then secondly, another reading of Scripture is too simple in that it renders too literal an interpretation of the promises to Israel in some OT passages. For we have also already seen how Paul deals with the fulfilment of the Abrahamic Covenant in Gal

3. See notably sessions 3 and 9.
4. See notably Q.14, in *LDL*, 88 and passim.

A Covenant Summary

3–4. Those three key things from Gen 12:1–3 become fascinatingly *reconfigured*, so that *the* descendant (rather than descendants, plural) becomes Jesus himself (v. 16), and the blessing becomes elided with the promised Holy Spirit (v. 14), which *together* constitute *the* inheritance, all received by means of faith (v. 18)—all given by the sheer grace of God and offered to *all* humankind, showing "no partiality" (Acts 10:34).[5]

The key to getting the balance between these two extremes right is to be found in the person of Jesus, Yahweh's faithful Servant and Messianic Son of God, in whom and in whom alone all the promises of God are fulfilled (2 Cor 1:18–20). For it is *from him* that *both* Jew *and* Gentile alike derive their true identity, becoming the people of God; there is now no essential distinction between these two groupings in the New Covenant (Gal 3:28, Eph 2:11–22). Indeed, we can go further and say that God's calling of *Israel/the Jews* in the first place was ever and only for the redemptive blessing of the *whole* (that's the literary logic of Genesis). But all of this does not then mean God has given up on the particular Jewish nation—"by no means!" The very point of Rom 9–11 is to speak of God's covenant faithfulness *as* the very basis of *anyone's hope*: this is the logic of the transition from Rom 8:17–39 and on into chapters 9–11. That is to say, there remains something yet to come for the ethnic people of Israel; but *what* exactly that something is, and *how* that is, and *when* that will be—all this, I suspect, will *surprise* us in the event, despite our very best speculations! For so it was when Jesus himself came the first time . . . ! In case you did not notice (reference again our "basic analogy," Q.9)!

At root therefore, on account of who Jesus himself is, both ethnic Israel and the church, comprised of both Gentiles and Messianic Jews, *are* "Israel"; for Jesus himself *is the* True Vine; and those who were afar off and those who are near, both are now reconstituted into the One New Human, Jesus, the *totus Christus*. That is, the church in space–time history derives its very identity via a figural reading of Scripture, both OT and NT together, such that it is able to "read" its own story, of blessing and curse, of failure

---

5. See notably session 9 on Galatians 3:1–4:7.

A Covenant Summary

and faithfulness, of forgetfulness and remembering, of suffering and glory, of repentance and redemption, precisely via the story of scriptural Israel itself, as it goes about its historical existence. And because that story of Israel is in fact not yet complete, with the mission of the worldwide pilgrim church called to witness to Jesus the Messiah of Israel among and to all the nations still *in via*, so too how exactly "all Israel will be saved" (Rom 11:26) remains to us "dim" (1 Cor 13:12, literally, "in a riddle") in the providence of God.[6]

---

6. A key resource to unraveling the complexities of the long tangled tale between church and synagogue is offered by Ephraim Radner, *Church*. See especially chapters 6 and 7, "The Church as Israel: The Repentant Missionary" and "The Figure of the Church."

A Way of "Reading" the Sacrament of the Eucharist

QUESTIONS 15 AND 16 from Session 5 alerted readers to the difficulties associated with various doctrines of Holy Communion/the Lord's Supper/the Eucharist/the Mass/the Divine Liturgy—we cannot even agree on a name! What follows is one of the most helpful ways I've found of disentangling this knotty issue. With acknowledgments to Donald Gelpi, *Charism and Sacrament*, 243–49.

There are three ways in which we use the word "appear[ance]," and how it both does and does not reflect our human grasp of "reality." The first, most direct and simple form goes like this.

1. A^1. Every morning the sun appears over the horizon. Another example: "Well officer; I was driving along quietly, when all of a sudden this car appeared from nowhere and hit us!" The point here is that previously something was hidden from sight (the sun, another car), and now our perceptions have engaged with a changed set of circumstances, pure and simple: it's day time, it's time to visit the panel beaters.

2. A^2. Every morning the sun appears (A^1) over the horizon. Yet what appears (A^2) *for those in the know* is an example of the solar system in action. Our simple perceptions from A^1 are now reconceptualized, by our bringing to bear upon our perceptions a larger frame of reference and understanding.

A Way of "Reading" the Sacrament of the Eucharist

In reality, the earth rotates about its axis every 24 hours, as it circles around the sun annually, along with all the other planets in the solar system, which too have their respective gyration and orbit speeds. What is vital here is the form in which we are now grasping the reality of the situation. We need to expand our understanding by somehow or other becoming "those who are in the know." Nor is this merely a case of sheer "progress" in human knowledge. Rather, such paradigm shifts are a combination of exercising faith, via the empirical, and the theoretical—of learning to view "reality" *from the point of view of* such-and-so, so that we now *view* it *as* such-and-so.[1]

3. A^3. The third way in which we use the idea of "appearance" also raises questions of interpretation and understanding as in A^2, but now things become intriguingly a case of "*only* appearances"—well; only at first sight! "Appearances can be deceptive," as we say. For example, should we place a stick in water, what was previously straight now suddenly appears (A^3) bent. Yet, on further inspection and greater reflection, what appears (A^2) *for those in the know* is an example of the refraction of light when it passes through a change in medium (from air to water in this case). Pull the stick out of the water—and behold, it becomes straight again! Put it back in, and it appears bent again!

The relevance of all this for how we may go about "reading" or appraising the sacrament of the Eucharist/Lord's Supper is this. All Christian Traditions are clear Jesus instituted something at the Last Supper with his disciples in the Upper Room. For my money, having spent many years with the literature from a number of traditions and having participated in a similar number of Christian communities' gatherings, I have concluded as follows. Brant Pitre's book, *Jesus and the Last Supper*, already noted, is I sense the

---

1. For those who wish to pursue this line of approach further, see McGrath, *The Science of God*. This is an introductory rewrite of his three volume *A Scientific Theology*. Polanyi's *Science, Faith and Society* is also most helpful.

very best at (re)situating what occurred and what it all conveyed in its original 1st century Jewish context. To be sure; the first few centuries of the church's history saw this sect within Judaism explode across the ancient Mediterranean world and beyond. And as it crossed boundaries in mission, boundaries geographical and cultural, the church down the centuries has appraised this liturgical meal in a variety of ways. Chapter 8 of *LDL* details something of this history.

The bottom line goes like this (see the summary in the right hand column under "continuation" of the Chart on page 89). The New Passover rite, transforming the old one commemorating the Exodus from Egypt (Exod 12–13) and instituted by Jesus in that Upper Room the night before he died, prophetically signals the reality of his New Covenant Promise to come and be present as the glorified Son of Man,[2] who offers to his gathered believers, the true, Living Bread from Heaven, which is his flesh for the life of the world, his body (a compressed paraphrase of John 6:32–58). In addition, from 1 Cor 10:16, we may see the Holy Spirit is the One who effects this *koinōnia* in Jesus' body and blood, this mutual indwelling (John 6:56), as and when the people of God gather in his Name, becoming God's temple.

As we saw in Part Three (and see *LDL*, chapter 8), only an adequate understanding of the ascended Jesus (who *is* the glorified Son of Man) pouring out the Holy Spirit upon his people to both initiate and maintain communion with and in his body (now a word with *double meaning*, as per 1 Cor 10–14) may truly enable any due sense of "church,"[3] and so ministry among or by the

---

2. We need to recall the Fourth Gospel's vital double entendre re divine glory being manifested in *both* crucifixion *and* resurrection.

3. See esp. Ziegler, *Trinitarian Grace*, for a beautiful analysis of God's personal gracious Presence through the Son and in the Holy Spirit. "Torrance's concept of grace ruthlessly refers to the personal self-giving movement of the triune God and the personal communion such a movement creates," xv, n.15. "The source of the Church determines the form of the Church. Because the Church is grounded 'in the self-communication of the Holy Trinity,' Torrance argues that any legitimate ecclesiology must make the trinitarian movement, 'from the Father, through the Son and in the Spirit, and to the Father, through the Son and in the Spirit,' the regulative center of all its worship, faith and

church. Those texts from Matthew, Mark, and Luke re the Last Supper, together with John 6 re the typical Johannine combination of "sign" and its explanation, the Upper Room discourses (John 13–17), and Paul in 1 Cor 5:6–8 and chapters 10–14—all these texts *school* Christians so that *they may be "in the know."* They may now *view* this rite *in a most particular way, as* more than might *appear* to be the case. Just so, Christians, *versed* in word-and-sacrament, Scripture-and-sign, may *view* their "taking, blessing, breaking, and distributing"[4] bread and wine to eat and drink—to *consume* them (the first Greek verb in John 6:54 is particularly strong)—when gathered together, *as* a key means of the triune God's realizing their participation in the Divine Life. No longer do the elements of bread and wine "appear" (A^3) only as mere material "creatures."[5] Instead, for those in the know, what "appears"(A^2), as the gathered church does all this, is the *realization* of the climax of the triune God's economy of salvation (in the life, death, resurrection, ascension of Jesus and the ensuing Gift of Pentecost),[6] and the opportunity for this singular God's gathered followers now to *renew* both their participation, their *koinōnia in* the One who fulfils that economy, and their due sacrifice of praise and thanksgiving *for* it all. As Karl Barth famously expressed it:

> χάρις (*charis*) always demands the answer of εὐχαριστία (*eucharistia*). Grace and gratitude belong together like heaven and earth. Grace evokes gratitude like the voice an echo. Gratitude follows grace like thunder lightening.[7]

---

mission," 188 (citing also *Trinitarian Faith*, 263).

4. This fourfold action or "shape" is seminally derived from the classic work of Dom Gregory Dix.

5. The language is that of Thomas Cranmer from the Anglican Book of Common Prayer.

6. Which phases of the history of salvation are often recited in those formal prayers of many a church tradition after the bread and wine are formally put on the table/altar.

7. *CD* IV/1, 41.

A Way of "Reading" the Sacrament of the Eucharist

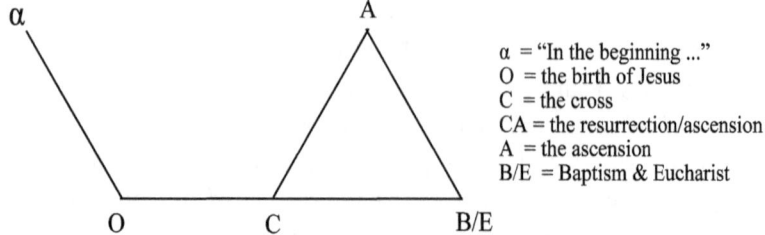

Figure 8: Luke–Acts revised displaying both dominical sacraments

Summary Chart of the One Baptism

Step One	Step Two	Step Three A	Step Three B	Step Three C	
Jesus Christ's career	Applied to us: Spirit Baptism	Our response	Our response	Sacramental expression/response	
				initiation	*continuation*
Conception and birth	Regeneration	Turn and become child-like		*1 "Be baptized"— a window on the spiritual reality viewed from *2 *Either of two places:* *1 or *2 infant or adult	"Do this to Remember Me" New Passover rite celebrating *koinōnia* in the Mediator of the New Exodus and the New Covenant, in the midst of the New Temple
Jordan					
Crucifixion	Crucified with Jesus	Put off/away Abstain— from the Old	Let yourselves be filled with the Holy Spirit		
Resurrection	Raised with Jesus	Put on Walk— the New Life			
Exaltation	Made to sit with Jesus	Put on armor and stand			

Bibliography

Suggestions for Further Reading

Balthasar, Hans Urs von, ed. *Spirit and Fire: A Thematic Anthology of the Writings of Origen.* Cornerstones. Translated by Robert J. Daly, SJ. London: Bloomsbury T&T Clark, 2nd ed. 2018.

Barth, Karl. *Church Dogmatics.* 4 vols. Edited by G. W. Bromiley and T. F. Torrance. Edinburgh: T & T Clark, 1956–75.

———. *Fifty Prayers.* Translated by David Carl Staasen. Louisville: Westminster John Knox, 2008.

Bartholomew, Craig G., and Michael W. Goheen. *The Drama of Scripture: Finding Your Place in the Biblical Story.* Grand Rapids: Baker Academic, 2004.

Bauckham, Richard. "Reading Scripture as a Coherent Story." In *The Art of Reading Scripture,* edited by Ellen F. Davis and Richard B. Hays, 38–53. Grand Rapids: Eerdmans, 2003.

Beale, G. K. *The Temple and the Church's Mission: A Biblical Theology of the Dwelling Place of God.* New Studies in Biblical Theology 17. Downers Grove, IL: IVP Academic, 2004.

Billings, J. Todd. *Union with Christ: Reframing Theology and Ministry for the Church.* Grand Rapids: Baker Academic, 2011.

Black, A. Bryden. *The Lion, the Dove, & the Lamb: An Exploration into the Nature of the Christian God as Trinity.* Eugene, OR: Wipf & Stock, rev. ed. 2018.

Bruce, F. F. *The Epistle to the Galatians: A Commentary on the Greek Text.* The New International Greek Testament Commentary. Exeter, England: Paternoster, 1982.

———. *This is That: The New Testament Development of Some Old Testament Themes.* Mount Radford Reprints 17. Exeter, England: Paternoster, 1976.

BIBLIOGRAPHY

———. *The Time is Fulfilled: Five Aspects of the Fulfillment of the Old Testament in the New*. Moore College Lectures, 1977. Exeter, England: Paternoster, 1978.

Brueggemann, Walter. *David's Truth in Israel's Imagination and Memory*. Philadelphia: Fortress, 1985.

———. *The Land: Place as Gift, Promise, and Challenge in Biblical Faith*. Overtures to Biblical Theology. London: SPCK, 1978.

Candler, Peter M., Jr. *Theology, Rhetoric, Manuduction, or Reading Scripture Together on the Path to God*. Radical Traditions: Theology in a Postcritical Key. Grand Rapids: Eerdmans, 2006.

Clements, Ronald E. *Old Testament Theology: A Fresh Approach*. London: Marshall, Morgan & Scott, 1978.

Clines, David J. A. *The Theme of the Pentateuch*. Journal for the Study of the Old Testament, Supplementary Series 10. Sheffield, England: Sheffield Academic, 2nd ed. 1997.

Dix, Gregory. *The Shape of the Liturgy*. London: Dacre, 1945.

Dunn, James D. G. *Baptism in the Holy Spirit*. Studies in Biblical Theology, Second Series 15. London: SCM, 1970.

Fee, Gordon D. *God's Empowering Presence: The Holy Spirit in the Letters of Paul*. Peabody, MA: Hendrickson, 1994.

Gelpi, Donald L., SJ. *Charism and Sacrament: A Theology of Christian Conversion*. London: SPCK, 1977.

Habel, Norman C. *The Land is Mine: Six Biblical Land Ideologies*. Overtures to Biblical Theology. Minneapolis: Fortress, 1995.

Hafemann, Scott J. *Suffering and Ministry in the Spirit: Paul's Defense of His Ministry in II Corinthians 2:14—3:3*. Grand Rapids: Eerdmans, 1990.

Hasel, Gerhard F. *Old Testament Theology: Basic Issues in the Current Debate*. Grand Rapids: Eerdmans, 4th ed. 1991.

Hays, Richard B. *Echoes of Scripture in the Gospels*. Waco: Baylor University Press, 2016.

———. *Echoes of Scripture in the Letters of Paul*. New Haven: Yale University Press, 1993.

———. *The Faith of Jesus Christ: The Narrative Substructure of Galatians 3:1—4:11*. The Biblical Resource Series. 2nd ed. Grand Rapids: Eerdmans, 2002.

———. *Reading Backwards: Figural Christology and the Fourfold Gospel Witness*. Waco: Baylor University Press, 2014.

Hendel, Ronald S. *Remembering Abraham: Culture, Memory, and History in the Hebrew Bible*. New York: Oxford University Press, 2005.

Hillers, Delbert R. *Covenant: The History of a Biblical Idea*. Seminars in the History of Ideas. Baltimore: Johns Hopkins University Press, 1969.

Horton, Michael. *Introducing Covenant Theology*. Grand Rapids: Baker, 2009.

Hurtado, Larry W. *Lord Jesus Christ: Devotion to Jesus in Earliest Christianity*. Grand Rapids: Eerdmans, 2003.

———. *One God, One Lord: Early Christian Devotion and Ancient Jewish Monotheism*. 3rd ed. London: T & T Clark, 2015.

Bibliography

Janzen, W. "Land." In *ABD* 4:143-54.

Jenson, Robert W. *Systematic Theology.* 2 vols. New York: Oxford University Press, 1997/99.

Jüngel, Eberhard. "The Emergence of the New." In *Theological Essays II*, translated by Arnold Neufeldt-Fast and J. B. Webster, and edited by J. B. Webster, 35-58. Edinburgh: T & T Clark, 1995.

Kline, Meredith G. *The Structure of Biblical Authority.* Grand Rapids: Eerdmans, revised ed. 1975.

Köstenberger, Andreas J., and Scott R. Swain. *Father, Son and Spirit: The Trinity and John's Gospel.* New Studies in Biblical Theology 24. Downers Grove, IL: IVP Academic, 2008.

Lewis, C. S. *The Last Battle: A Story for Children.* Harmondsworth, England: Penguin, 1964.

Lubac, Henri Cardinal de, SJ. "Spiritual Understanding." Translated by Luke O'Neill. In *The Theological Interpretation of Scripture: Classic and Contemporary Readings*, edited by Stephen E. Fowl, 3-25. Blackwell Readings in Modern Theology. Oxford: Blackwell, 1997.

Marion, Jean-Luc. *In The Self's Place: The Approach of Saint Augustine.* Translated by Jeffrey L. Kosky. Stanford: Stanford University Press, 2012.

McGrath, A. E. *Luther's Theology of the Cross: Martin Luther's Theological Breakthrough.* 2nd ed. Chichester, England: Wiley-Blackwell, 2011.

———. *The Science of God: An Introduction to Scientific Theology.* Grand Rapids: Eerdmans, 2004.

———. *A Scientific Theology, vol.1 nature, vol.2 reality, vol.3 theory.* Grand Rapids: Eerdmans, 2001/2/3.

McKenna, John H. *Eucharist and Holy Spirit: The eucharistic epiclesis in twentieth century theology (1900-1966).* Alcuin Club Collections No. 57. Great Wakering, Essex: Mayhew-McCrimmon, 1975.

Pate, C. Marvin, et al. *The Story of Israel. A Biblical Theology.* Downers Grove, IL: IVP Academic, 2004.

Perrin, Nicholas. *Jesus the Temple.* Grand Rapids: Baker Academic, 2010.

Pitre, Brant. *Jesus and the Last Supper.* Grand Rapids: Eerdmans, 2015.

Polanyi, Michael. *Science, Faith and Society.* Chicago: University of Chicago Press, 1964.

Radner, Ephraim. *Church.* Eugene, OR: Cascade, 2017.

Rahner, Karl. *The Trinity.* Translated by Joseph Donceel. London: Burns & Oates, 1970.

Rhodes, Jonty. *Covenants Made Simple: Understanding God's Unfolding Promises to His People.* Phillipsburg, NJ: P & R Publishing, 2014.

Ribbens, Benjamin J. "Typology of Types: Typology in Dialogue." In *Journal of Theological Interpretation*, 5 (2011) 81-95.

Sanders, Fred. *The Triune God.* New Studies in Dogmatics. Grand Rapids: Zondervan, 2016.

Schmemann, Alexander. *The Eucharist: Sacrament of the Kingdom.* Translated by Paul Kachur. New York: St. Vladimir's Seminary, 1987.

Bibliography

———. *Of Water and the Spirit*. London: SPCK, 1976.
Selwyn, E. G. *The First Epistle of St. Peter: The Greek Text with Introduction, Notes and Essays*. 2nd ed. London: MacMillan, 1947.
Soulen, R. Kendall. *The Divine Name(s) and the Holy Trinity, vol. 1 Distinguishing the Voices*. Louisville: WJK, 2011.
Swain, Scott R. *Trinity, Revelation, and Reading: A Theological Introduction to the Bible and its Interpretation*. London: Bloomsbury T&T Clark, 2011.
Torrance, T. F. "The Mind of Christ in Worship: The Problem of Apollinarianism in the Liturgy." In *Theology in Reconciliation: Essays Towards Evangelical and Catholic Unity in East and West*, 139–214. London: Geoffrey Chapman, 1975.
———. "The One Baptism Common to Christ and His Church. In *Theology in Reconciliation: Essays Towards Evangelical and Catholic Unity in East and West*, 82–105. London: Geoffrey Chapman, 1975.
———. "The Paschal Mystery of Christ and the Eucharist." In *Theology in Reconciliation: Essays Towards Evangelical and Catholic Unity in East and West*, 106–38. London: Geoffrey Chapman, 1975.
———. *Theology in Reconciliation: Essays Towards Evangelical and Catholic Unity in East and West*. London: Geoffrey Chapman, 1975.
Vickers, Jason E. *Invocation and Assent: The Making and Remaking of Trinitarian Theology*. Grand Rapids: Eerdmans, 2008.
Webster, John. *Holy Scripture: A Dogmatic Sketch*. Current Issues in Theology 1. Cambridge: Cambridge University Press, 2003.
———. "One Who Is Son: Theological Reflections on the Exordium to the Epistle to the Hebrews." In *The Epistle to the Hebrews and Christian Theology*, edited by Richard Bauckham et al., 69–94. Grand Rapids: Eerdmans, 2009.
Wright, Christopher J. H. *God's People in God's Land: Family, Land, and Property in the Old Testament*. Grand Rapids: Eerdmans, 1990.
Wright, N. T. *Christian Origins and the Question of God*. Vol. 1, *The New Testament and the People of God*. London: SPCK, 1992.
———. *Christian Origins and the Question of God*. Vol. 2, *Jesus and the Victory of God*. London: SPCK, 1996.
———. *Christian Origins and the Question of God*. Vol. 3, *The Resurrection of the Son of God*. London: SPCK, 2003.
Young, Frances, and David F. Ford. *Meaning and Truth in 2 Corinthians*. Biblical Foundations in Theology. London: SPCK, 1987.
Ziegler, Geordie W. *Trinitarian Grace and Participation: An Entry into the Theology of T. F. Torrance*. Minneapolis: Fortress, 2017.

www.ingramcontent.com/pod-product-compliance
Lightning Source LLC
Chambersburg PA
CBHW080426210426
R18171700001B/R181717PG43193CBX00039B/65